C

with

EXCELLENCE

fff

HOWARD W. SAMS & COMPANY
HAYDEN BOOKS

Related Titles

Advanced C Primer++
Stephen Prata, The Waite Group

**C Programmer's Guide
to Serial Communications**
Joe Campbell

MS-DOS® Bible
Steven Simrin, The Waite Group

Discovering MS-DOS®
Kate O'Day, The Waite Group

MS-DOS® Developer's Guide
*John Angermeyer and Kevin Jaeger,
The Waite Group*

Tricks of the MS-DOS® Masters
*John Angermeyer, Rich Fahringer,
Kevin Jaeger, and Dan Shafer, The Waite Group*

Inside XENIX®
Christopher L. Morgan, The Waite Group

UNIX® Primer Plus
*Mitchell Waite, Donald Martin,
and Stephen Prata, The Waite Group*

**Advanced UNIX® —
A Programmer's Guide**
Stephen Prata, The Waite Group

UNIX® Shell Programming Language
Rod Manis and Marc Meyer

UNIX® System V Bible
*Stephen Prata and Donald Martin,
The Waite Group*

**UNIX® System V Primer,
Revised Edition**
*Mitchell Waite, Stephen Prata,
and Donald Martin, The Waite Group*

**C Primer Plus,
Revised Edition**
*Mitchell Waite, Stephen Prata,
and Donald Martin, The Waite Group*

Turbo C Programming for the IBM
*Robert Lafore, The Waite Group
(forthcoming)*

Quick C Programming
*Carl Townsend
(forthcoming)*

UNIX® Communications
Bryan Costales, The Waite Group

VM/CMS Handbook
Howard Fosdick

Hayden Books
UNIX System Library

UNIX® Shell Programming
Stephen G. Kochan and Patrick H. Wood

UNIX® System Security
Patrick H. Wood and Stephen G. Kochan

UNIX® System Administration
David Fiedler and Bruce H. Hunter

Exploring the UNIX® System
Stephen G. Kochan and Patrick H. Wood

UNIX® Text Processing
Dale Dougherty and Tim O'Reilly

Programming in C
Stephen G. Kochan

Topics in C Programming
Stephen G. Kochan and Patrick H. Wood

*For the retailer nearest you, or to order directly from the publisher,
call 800-428-SAMS. In Indiana, Alaska, and Hawaii call 317-298-5699.*

C
with
EXCELLENCE
Programming Proverbs

HENRY F. LEDGARD
with JOHN TAUER

HAYDEN BOOKS

A Division of Howard W. Sams & Company
4300 West 62nd Street
Indianapolis, Indiana 46268 USA

International Standard Book Number: *0-672-46294-X*
Library of Congress Catalog Card Number: *87-60648*

Acquisitions Editor: *Michael Violano*
Editor: *Louis Keglovits*
Interior Designer: *T. R. Emrick*
Cover Illustration: *Keni Hill, Meridian Design Studio Inc.*
Composition: *Photo Comp Corp., Brownsburg, IN*

Printed in the United States of America

LightspeedC is a trademark of THINK Technologies, Inc.

CONTENTS

FOREWORD

To the original edition of *Programming Proverbs*,
Hayden Books, 1975

By necessity, computer science, computer education, and computer practice are all embryonic human activities, for they have existed for only a single generation. From the beginning, programming has been a frustrating black art, with individual abilities ranging from the excellent to the ridiculous and often exhibiting very little in the way of systematic mental procedure. In a sense, the teaching of programming through mistakes and debugging can hardly be regarded as legitimate university-level course work. At the university level we teach such topics as the notion of an algorithm, concepts in programming languages, compiler design, operating systems, information storage and retrieval, artificial intelligence, and numerical computation; but in order to implement ideas in any of these functional activities, we need to write programs in a specific language.

Students and professionals alike tend to be overly optimistic about their ability to write programs or to make programs work according to preestablished design goals. However, we are beginning to see a breakthrough in programming as a mental process. This breakthrough is based more on considerations of style than on detail. It involves taking style seriously, not only in how programs look when they are completed, but in the very mental processes that create them. In programming, it is not enough to be inventive and ingenious. One also needs to be disciplined and controlled in order not to become entangled in one's own complexities.

In any new area of human activity, it is difficult to foresee latent human capabilities. We have many examples of such capabilities: touch typing, speed writing, and 70-year-old grandmothers who drive down our highways at 70 miles an hour. Back in 1900, it was possible to foresee cars going 70 miles an hour, but the drivers were imagined as daredevils rather than as grandmothers. The moral is that in any new human activity one generation hardly scratches the surface of its capabilities. So it will be in programming as well.

The next generation of programmers will be much more competent than the first one. They will have to be. Just as it was easier to get into college in the "good old days," it was also easier to get by as a programmer in the "good old days." For this new generation, a programmer will need to be capable of a level of precision and productivity never dreamed of before.

This new generation of programmers will need to acquire discipline and control, mainly by learning to write programs correctly from the start. The debugging process will take the new form of verifying that no errors are present, rather than the old form of finding and fixing errors over and over (otherwise known as "acquiring confidence by exhaustion"). Programming is a serious logical business that requires concentration and precision. In this discipline, concentration is highly related to confidence.

In simple illustration, consider a child who knows how to play a perfect game of tic-tac-toe but does not know that he knows. If you ask him to play for something important, like a candy bar, he will say to himself, "I hope I can win." And sometimes he will win, and sometimes not. The only reason he does not always win is that he drops his concentration. He does not realize this fact because he regards winning as a chance event. Consider how different the situation is when the child *knows* that he knows how to play a perfect game of tic-tac-toe. Now he does not say, "I hope I can win." He says instead, "I know I can win; it's up to me!" And he recognizes the necessity for concentration in order to ensure that he wins.

In programming, as in tic-tac-toe, it is characteristic that concentration goes hand in hand with justified confidence in one's own ability. It is not enough simply to know how to write programs correctly. The programmer must *know that he knows* how to write programs correctly, and then supply the concentration to match.

This book of proverbs is well suited to getting members of the next generation off to the right start. The elements of style discussed here can help provide the mental discipline to master programming complexity. In essence, the book can help a programmer make a large first step on the road to a new generation of programming.

HARLAN D. MILLS
Federal Systems Division, IBM
Gaithersburg, Maryland

PREFACE

C is a programming language that evokes strong reactions. I have heard many passing remarks. They run roughly like this:

- C is the language of choice.
- C is the alternative to assembler language.
- C is for "real" software, i.e., systems programming.
- The speed is it.
- The syntax is dreadful.
- It's a hacker's language.
- C is wonderful.

While I have my own reservations about the syntax of C, the language has achieved a notable status. There seems little doubt that its ability to promote systems programming and avoid assembler language is a major achievement.

Many years ago the first version of the "Programming Proverbs" appeared. This work was motivated by a small book called *The Elements of Style*, written by William Strunk, Jr., and revised by E. B. White. Originally conceived in 1918, Strunk's book stressed the need for rigor, conciseness, and clarity in the writing of English prose. In like manner, this C version of the Proverbs is intended for C programmers who want to write carefully constructed, readable programs.

Over the years much has been learned about programming. Each successive version of the Programming Proverbs has incorporated this knowledge. Each version has been improved both in form and content. Nevertheless, writing this version in C has not been easy. Two factors stood out:

- Efficiency is a vital part of C, and this can get in the way of readability.

- The syntax of the language, in several places, resists clarity.

It is fine to say that Construct A is clearer than Construct B, but if Construct B is hardly efficient or so unusual in C, the justification of Construct B is seriously weakened.

The dilemma, though, is even deeper. The need for clarity is especially great in C. The C language is system oriented and thus is used for "real" software, that is, software maintained for years. C programmers should put craftsmanship and elegance as a primary design goal. Unfortunately, the power of C is often misdirected, excuses are made, and impenetrable code is often written.

This book is designed not as an introduction to the details of C, but as a guide to better programming. It should be of value to all programmers who have some familiarity with C. As such, it may be used as a supplement in courses where C programming is a major concern, or as an informal guide to those who have an interest in improving software quality.

I strongly believe that the ideas presented should go hand in hand with learning the C language itself. The reader who dismisses the overall objective of this book with the comment, "I've got to learn all about C first," may be surprised to find that the study of good programming practices in conjunction with the basics of the language may reap quick and longstanding rewards.

C with Excellence is organized in three major parts. After the opening statement of the Introduction, Part One gives a collection of simple rules, called *proverbs*. The proverbs summarize in terse form the major ideas of this book.

Part Two elaborates on several important and sometimes controversial ideas discussed in the chapter on programming proverbs. It includes a chapter on program standards, giving the programming conventions used in this book. These rules have been strictly followed here.

Part Three captures the point of the entire text with an example of a strict top-down approach to a programming problem. The approach is oriented toward the easy writing of complete, correct, readable programs. The approach hinges on developing the overall logical structure of the program first. Moreover, the programming proverbs are brought into action during the program's development. This chapter concludes with a full-scale program, given in Appendix B. The program is intended as a model of good programming.

As mentioned above, this work is based on several predecessors, the so-called "Programming Proverbs" series: *Programming Proverbs, Programming Proverbs for FORTRAN Programmers, Cobol with Style, BASIC with Style, FORTRAN with Style, Pascal with Style*, and, notably, *Pascal with Excellence*. Many people assisted or inspired these earlier works, including William Cave, Leslie Chaikin, Louis Chmura, Joseph Davison, William Fastie, Jon Hueras, Michael Marcotty, Paul Nagin, and Andrew Singer.

Frank Lhota helped me start this C version. Mitch Gart deserves a special bow. He explained the inner logic of C to me, answered my odd questions, and has a gift in explaining things quietly and well. Stephen Kochan offered a thoughtful, professional review of this work.

The motivation for doing this current work owes much to my experience in teaching professional programmers for full-time seven-week courses at Philips Electronics in Europe. These courses were under the brilliant direction of Allen Macro, assisted by John Buxton. The participants in the courses, together with my colleague Nat Macon, deepened my commitment to excellence.

The programs given here follow the commonly accepted version of C. For a definition of the common basis of C, see the ANSI standard definition of C. The programs given here were run with THINK Technologies *LightspeedC* on the Macintosh. For a good tutorial on C with a good sense of craftsmanship, I recommend *A book on C* [Kelley and Pohl, 1984].

C with excellence is basically my own personal statement about programming. There are likely to be things you disagree with. But, above all else, I firmly believe that the study of guidelines for good programming can be of great value to all programmers and that there are principles that transcend the techniques of any individual practitioner.

Henry Ledgard
RFD 3
Amherst, MA 01002

TO THE READER

In a profession where change is the order of the day, programmers tend to be thrown off the foundations over which the profession was built. We rush for solutions often before we examine the problem in depth. Sometimes we succeed. But we pay a price. The price is software that is far from excellent, both in its user interface and its underlying quality.

This book is a two-fold response to these observations. First, the programming proverbs represent years of thinking about some basic issues. This is a substantive work, about issues that count.

And second, this work is lighthearted in many ways. The approach is not directed away from the technical issues but toward conveying key ideas with good spirit. The purpose is to teach the fledgling and (I hope) remind the veteran that certain principles need to be reviewed now and again.

PART
ONE

PROGRAMMING PROVERBS

INTRODUCTION

I have seen the future, and it works.

Lincoln Steffens

Whenever anyone discusses the "state of the art" in a discipline or profession, the purpose is to make a statement of what "is" to what "can be" or what "ought to be." This was an inherent objective of the earlier editions of the Programming Proverbs Series. Now, many years later, it is somewhat disheartening for me to report that what "was" still "is."

Seldom are the results of a programming development project concluded with a proud exclamation: "It worked right the first time!" That programs seldom work right the first time is not the only indication of the state of the art. Sometimes programs work only part of the time, some never work at all. Of the ones that do, their utility is lost in the arduous and often painful effort to maintain them. Writing high-quality programs is possible, but unusual. I ask the question: Why is the product program so poor so often, i.e., why don't programmers succeed more often? The reasons are simple. First, programming is difficult, especially as programmers must keep pace with an expanding and demanding technology—ours is a profession that is never static, even from one project to the next.

Second, there are very few principles for developing and writing good programs. We tend to think that the principles of programming lie in the perfection and execution of the algorithm itself and, once we have learned the programming language, all that needs to be known is understood. The result is that programmers conceive procedures to work around the difficulties of programming—procedures that are often born in the heat of development—but they have few *principles* to rely upon for real success.

The concern of the computer industry about the quality of software has persisted for many years. Surely the time has come for programmers to write programs that work correctly the first time—or at least the tenth or twentieth time—programs that do the job even when the original problem was poorly conceived; programs that are easy to read, understand, and maintain.

Some may think attempts to correct such practices are unrealistic, especially considering their past experiences of constant revision, debugging, and difficulties in deciphering code. There are, however, well-founded principles that can be utilized to achieve these goals. Some of these principles I shall present are obvious, even to novice programmers. Others, even experienced programmers might debate. However, before any principle is rejected, it must be remembered that a program is not only a set of descriptions and instructions for a computer, but *a document that must be understood by human beings*—for you, the programmer first of all, and for all others who will read your program in the process from development to maintenance.

It is well known that the cost of program development and maintenance is high and growing higher. In fact, I have heard it said that the cost of program maintenance on some poorly constructed systems is a hundred times greater than the cost of initial development and testing. To attack these costs, methodology and clarity must be early programming concerns.

Although the development of effective algorithms and data structures is an important activity that is closely related to general programming techniques, this is not the focus here. The issue here is how to help the programmer write clear programs of impeccable quality. With this in mind, the programming proverbs are the motivation for this book.

As with most maxims or proverbs the rules are not absolute, but neither are they arbitrary. Each proverb is a reservoir of thought and experience. At first glance, some of them may seem trivial or too time-consuming to follow. But they were written to be succinct and useful, much (I hope) like Ben Franklin's simple maxims that he collected as a guide to everyday living in his *Poor Richard's Almanac*. Like old saws, the proverbs overlook much important detail in favor of easily remembered phrases. Indeed, there are some cases where programs should not conform to

Figure 1. **Matrix summary of The Programming Proverbs**

	DEV	DOC	CODE	TEST	DEBUG	M&M
Chapter 1. *A Good Start Is Half the Race*						
1 Don't Panic	★★					
2 Question the Problem	★★	★				
3 Define the Problem	★	★★	★			★
4 Document First	★	★★★	★			★
5 Think First, Code Later			★★★	★		★
6 Proceed Top-Down			★	★	★	★★★
7 Beware of Other Approaches			★★		★	★
Chapter 2. *Structure Is Logic*						
8 Code It for the Other Guy			★		★★	★★★
9 Don't Nest					★	★
10 Black-Box Your Subroutines				★★	★★★	★★★
11 Don't Goto			★		★	★
Chapter 3. *Coding the Program*						
12 All Words Mean Something			★★		★	★★
13 Spaces Have Meaning, Too			★		★	★★
14 Comment for Content				★		★
15 Make Constants Constant			★★			★★
16 Name All Types			★		★	★
17 Get the Syntax Correct Now			★★			
18 Remember Your Reader						★★★
19 Your Output Is Not Only for You		★		★★		
20 Review, Review, Review				★	★	★
21 Careful Programmers Don't Have Accidents				★	★	
Chapter 4. *And of Course . . .*						
22 Have Someone Else Read the Work	★★	★★	★★	★★	★★	★★★
23 What Have You Read Lately?	★★	★★				
24 Don't Be Afraid to Start Over				★★	★★	
Total	**10**	**11**	**20**	**13**	**18**	**30**

Note: The stars indicate my subjective evaluation of the relative values of the processes indicated.

standard rules—that is, there are exceptions to every proverb. Nevertheless, I think experience will show that these exceptions are rare and that a programmer should not violate these rules without serious reasons to do so.

A list of the proverbs is given in Figure 1. The proverbs are further related to a relative timing process of development (DEV), documentation (DOC), coding (CODE), testing (TEST), debugging (DEBUG), and maintenance and modification (M&M). This figure suggests their relative impact on programming.

The relative importance of one proverb over another depends quite markedly on the problem at hand. By assigning a relative value to each proverb based on observation and experience (as in Figure 1), the graph in Figure 2 indicates the overall effect of the proverbs during program development.

In closing this introduction, note that the word "proverb" is used, rather than the most accurate word "maxim." Proverbs and maxims both refer to pithy sayings derived from practical experience. Proverbs are usually well known, whereas maxims are not. Admittedly, the programming proverbs are not in themselves popular sayings. However, the title was chosen with an idea to the future. I hope that these proverbs will assist programmers in joining Lincoln Steffens in seeing the future with the confidence that it will work.

Figure 2   *Overall impact of the proverbs*

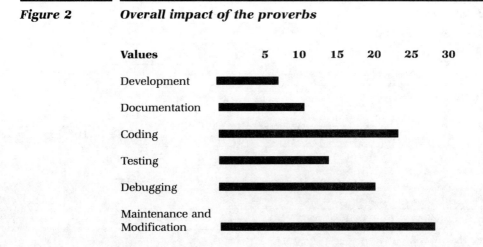

6

CHAPTER

1 *A GOOD START IS HALF THE RACE*

First establish the main principles and the small details cannot get away.

Mencius
Cofounder of Confucianism

Proverb 1   ***DON'T PANIC***   *The world belongs to the enthusiast who keeps cool.*
WILLIAM MCFEE
Casuals of the Sea, Book I

Most programming projects are the result of a need for a new piece of software to solve a new problem or the need to modify and improve a functioning piece of software. There should be a thoughtful prelude to the project, but at the moment of inception, panic begins to reign when reason is needed most. The causes are as varied as the personalities that attend them. More often than not, a programmer is loaded down with other work of equal importance. Instructors or management may put pressure on you by setting an unrealistic schedule. You may need to finish before the semester ends, or there may be a bonus for completing by some deadline. There is a tendency for the enthusiastic programmer to "get on with the job," i.e., code, code, code. Overlooking this first programming proverb results in a tendency to obtain speedy results—this is counter to all good programming practices.

Good sense must prevail. The same thoughtful approach that defined the project must be carried into the initial phases of the project before coding is begun. To rush in panic to the terminal will surely result in a situation that is all too common today,

7

where existing code must constantly be reworked as new code shows oversights, where bugs hide all over the finished code, and maintenance takes longer than expected.

This advice applies to programmers and project managers alike: if you find yourself plowing ahead with a new programming assignment, don't panic.

1. Stop.

2. Calm down.

3. Return to methodical programming techniques that work.

Time is your ally. Sometimes, if the enthusiast takes the afternoon off, he or she will discover what can be done in the cool of the evening.

Proverb 2

QUESTION THE PROBLEM

Programmers must recognize the difference between solving a puzzle and solving a programming problem. There is only one solution to a puzzle, but a problem often comes begging its own definition. A puzzle may be simply rearranging pieces on a card table until the picture stands before us; it may be finding the elusive definition that fills in the last square of a crossword. But a programming problem asks the examiner to question the premise of the problem itself.

More often than not, programmers are handed a problem to be solved—not a puzzle to be solved. Someone else invents the problem. Most likely, there will be a written description of the problem. The first impulse is to take the problem as stated. Watch out! This is the difference between a puzzle and a problem.

There are two almost universal difficulties with the statement of a problem or, as it is usually referred to, the "specification" of a problem:

1. The problem is not fully specified. There may be gaping omissions and inconsistencies.

2. The problem itself can be better defined.

This proverb addresses the second point.

Consider the small problem definition of Figure 1-1A. It is set in type, looks unnegotiable, and may even seem reasonable. Stop. Why do the inputs need to be in columns? As stated,

```
20000  8.00    22-1
```

is a fine input, but

```
20000 8.00 22 -1
```

is not. Thus, input is tedious and error prone. And why -1, not a "?" or -9? How will the computer read -1 when (say, for the percentage) a fixed-point real number is requested? And who will remember the order of inputs? How will the user know what to input? For a small problem, this is a fast start to trouble.

Figure 1-1B gives a more inspired problem definition. The difference may not seem great, but it is certainly better for the human user, and probably easier to implement as well.

Figure 1-1.   ***Proposed definitions of a mortgage problem***

(A) Poor Problem Definition

We wish to devise a program to help potential homeowners assess the finances of mortgaging a home. There are four basic factors to be considered: the principal, the interest rate, the number of years for the mortgage, and the monthly payment. The program must input values for any three of the above quantities, output the fourth quantity, and also output a table indicating how the amount of the first monthly payment of each year is divided between principal and interest.

The input to this program is a line containing three of the above four figures:

Columns	Quantity
1-5	Principal
8-12	Interest Rate
15-16	Number of years
17-23	Monthly payments

The principal and number of years are given as integers, the interest rate and monthly payments are given as fixed-point real numbers. The missing quantity is given as -1.

The output is to be a line indicating the value of the missing quantity, and a table giving, for the first monthly payment of each year, the amount contributed to decreasing the principal and the amount paid as interest.

(B) Better Problem Definition

We wish to devise a program to help potential homeowners assess the finances of mortgaging a home. There are four basic factors to be considered: the principal, the interest rate, the number of years for the mortgage, and the monthly payment. The program must obtain values for any three of the above quantities, output the fourth quantity, and also output a table indicating how the amount of the first monthly payment of each year is divided between principal and interest.

The program will prompt the user for the following four figures:

Quantity	Prompt
Principal	Enter Principal (in whole dollars):
Number of years	Enter Loan Period (in whole years):
Interest rate	Enter Interest Rate (to two decimal places):
Monthly payment	Enter Monthly Payment (to two decimal places):

The principal and number of years are given as integers, the interest rate and monthly payments are given as fixed-point real numbers. The missing quantity is given as zero.

The output is to be a line indicating the value of the missing quantity, and a table giving, for the first monthly payment of each year, the amount contributed to decreasing the principal and the amount paid as interest.

The miniature example above is not the odd case. Specifications written for programs will astound you! For instance:

1. Far too many features

2. Unreadable prose

3. Confusing inputs or outputs

4. Baroque syntax for user notations

5. Overly complex solutions

6. Lack of thought to new versions

7. Strange punctuations for user notations

8. Impossible scheduling requirements

9. Cryptic messages

10. Etc., etc., etc.

You cannot be discouraged. Your task is simply to question the problem that was given to you—it is not a puzzle, it is a problem . . . it comes with the territory. I have seen all these "problems with problems." Don't let them happen to you.

You should be reminded of John Stuart Mill's classic remark more than a hundred years ago:

> To question all things; - never to turn away from any difficulty; to accept no doctrine either from ourselves or from other people without a rigid scrutiny . . . these are the lessons we learn . . .

Questioning a problem in programming is, indeed, the lesson you must learn.

Proverb 3   **DEFINE THE PROBLEM**   *Nothing is difficult to a man who has persistence.*
CHINESE PROVERB

Once satisfied with the rough specifications of a problem, you must tackle the task of defining the problem completely. This and the previous proverb are, perhaps, one: as you question the problem, the definition of the problem will become clear to you. Good problem definitions are vital to the construction of good programs. An incomplete or ill-formed definition implies that the problem is not fully understood. Missing information, ignorance of special cases, and an abundance of extraneous information in a definition are good signs of poor programs or, at best, of programs that will be a surprise for the ultimate user. Any program that processes large amounts of data is bound to encounter some simple unnoticed condition, resulting in the all too common program crash.

We have often heard the claim that it is quite permissible to start with an imperfect problem definition, for during later program development a good programmer will readily pick up any critical points missed in the initial definition. This is a dangerous premise as it is counter to all the principles of professional programming. Starting with solid, complete program definition is laborious and requires persistence. But it is often half the solution to the entire problem. Moreover, good definitions will serve as the basis for good program documentation, and make programming itself easier.

There are many reasons why precise problem definitions are rare. First, there is no well-accepted idea of what comprises a precise definition. Different programmers, instructors, and managers usually employ different definition techniques. For example, some project managers require only program narratives, decision tables, or system flowcharts. Another common practice is to have an experienced systems analyst draw up several system flowcharts, some narrative descriptions, and some detailed descriptions of some inputs and outputs. Of course, the quality and completeness of these definitions will vary according to the style of the individual analyst.

Second, as we noted in the first proverb, there is an almost irresistible temptation to skirt over the issue of definition in order to "get on with the job." This temptation is especially acute when the given problem is similar to previously solved problems or when there is strong external pressure to produce some quick, visible results (that is, programs). Furthermore, even if programmers could avoid the rush to get on with the job, management and the "customer" often make it difficult to invest the time and money in a good problem definition. The results of good definitions often appear to be wasted, since working code is usually delayed, especially when a programmer works hard to ensure that no problem situations go unnoticed.

Third, good problem definitions involve plain hard work. There is an intense amount of persistence and discipline required to get any definition straight.

As an example, consider the earlier definition of Figure 1-1B, which defined a program to aid a prospective homeowner in determining the financial arrangements of a mortgage loan. The definition might appear adequate, but on closer analysis many points need to be resolved:

1. How are the principal, number of years, interest rate, and monthly payments related? Is there a formula?

2. Where are the prompts?

3. Are the ranges for each value adequate?

4. What input errors can arise?

5. Why can't we see a sample of the input/output?

6. What is the format of the table?

7. Does the table have headings?

8. Are numbers like "20,000" allowed?

These decisions will have to be made eventually. Now is the time. The definition in Figure 1-2 resolves each of the above issues. Although longer, it is more precise than that of Figure 1-1B.

One important point of Figure 1-2 is the inclusion of a sample of the input and output. Often a simple dialogue or printout can be of great value to a program in giving a quick synopsis of the problem. In addition, a sample can prevent surprises in cases where the program turns out to be quite different from the expectations of the person defining the program. If a programmer is not given a sample of the input-output, he or she should try to provide it before programming. It is a pity that samples are so rarely done, as though we in our own trade are hiding from the real problems we are committed to solve.

Figure 1-2.   *Clarified definition of a mortgage problem*

(1) *Problem Outline*: We wish to devise a program to help potential homeowners assess the finances of mortgaging a home. There are four basic quantities to be considered:

13

P   The principal amount of the mortgage
I   The yearly interest rate for the mortgage
N   The number of years for the duration of the mortgage
M   The constant monthly payment required to pay back the principal P over N years at the interest rate I.

The above quantities are related by the equation:

$$M = \frac{P * i * (1 + i)^n}{(i + i)^n - 1}$$

where

i = I/12 = monthly interest rate
n = 12*N = number of monthly periods in N years.

Briefly, the program is to input any three of the above quantities, compute and print the fourth quantity, and also print a table specifying how the first monthly payment of each year is divided between interest and principal.

(2) *Input*: The program will prompt the user for the values of P, N, I, and M. These have the general form:

P: ddddd
N: dd
I: dd.dd
M: ddd.dd

where the d's represent decimal digits such that

P = the principal in dollars
N = the number of years in integer form
I   = the percentage interest rate computed to two decimal places
M = the monthly payment in dollars and cents.

The value of P, I, N, or M to be computed is given as zero. Additional or fewer digits (than those shown above) are allowed. However, each whole number must have at least one digit, and each decimal point number must have at least one digit on each side of the decimal point. Except to the right of a decimal point, leading zeros may be replaced by blanks.

(3) *Output*: The output from the program is to consist of two parts: (a) The value to be computed, using one of the formats:

```
PRINCIPAL            = $dddddd
NUMBER OF YEARS    = dd
INTEREST RATE      = dd.dd
MONTHLY PAYMENT = $dddd.dd
```

(b) A table giving for the first monthly payment of each year the amount paid to principal and the amount paid to interest. The headings and formats for the table values are as follows:

YEAR	AMT TO PRINCIPAL	AMT TO INTEREST
dd	$ddd.dd	$ddd.dd

Except to the right of a decimal point, leading zeros for any value are to be replaced by blanks.

(4) *Exceptional Conditions*: If any of the input values are not in the prescribed format, the user is to be prompted for the value again. If any output value is not in the range indicated, the program is to print an appropriate message to the user.

(5) *Sample Input*:

The principal, number of years, interest rate, and monthly payment of a mortgage are required below. Enter three values, and enter 0 for the value to be computed.

```
Enter principal (in whole dollars): 20000
Enter loan period (in whole years): 25
Enter interest rate (to two decimal places): 8.0%
** Value not recognized. Try again: 8.00
Enter monthly payment (to two decimal places): 0
```

(6) *Sample Output for Above Input*:

MONTHLY PAYMENT = $154.36

YEAR	AMT TO PRINCIPAL	AMT TO INTEREST
1	21.03	133.33
2	22.77	131.59
⋮		
25	142.53	11.83

In Chapter 7, we will discuss several ideas for producing good problem definitions in conjunction with a complete example. However, there are a few points about good definitions that deserve to be mentioned here. First, in attempting to supply a complete problem definition, the programmer probably cannot err by devoting extra time and thought. While perfect definitions are probably unattainable, with good technique and discipline, you will end up "close" to one. Remember that all languages have rigid rules for the execution of programs, and programmers must be specific to the last detail. If something is left unspecified in the original definition, the programmer will eventually have to face the consequences. At best, the changes that must be made are frustrating and distracting.

Once you believe that a definition is complete, put it aside for a while. Pick it up later, reread and rethink it—this is genuine persistence. Better still, have someone else read it (see Proverb 22). The problem definitions thought to be "complete" may reveal flaws by the light of a new day or the cool of another evening. You will find that most of these proverbs apply simultaneously to any problem you have. As a final word, make sure that you have a complete written description of the problem before you do anything else.

Proverb 4   ## *DOCUMENT FIRST*

What can be said in one short proverb about a subject that has been cussed and discussed for years? Many have tried to define and analyze program documentation, to motivate programmers to understand that the central purpose of documentation is to provide effective communication of factual information among people. The most important aspect of documentation is not just to do it early, but to do it first. You will be in close touch with your user's or instructor's requirements so that your understanding of the required program will be greatly enhanced.

What is "documentation" in the sense that we define it here? It could be:

a. In a class exercise, a summary of program design.

b. In a class project, a manual or write-up of how to use the program.

c. In a commercial project, a reference manual or user's guide.

d. In a contracted piece of software, an installation manual or user's guide.

Very often, it comes down to:

a. The comments at the beginning of a program.

b. The user manual.

Now, very few programmers do these things before coding. Why?

Because documentation takes effort. And because, more often than not, it appears to be a drudgery. It is easy to hide from hard work, to consider it premature if not impossible. Rubbish.

There is quite a difference between 'I can't do it' and 'I won't do it'. Usually it is the latter.

MENCIUS

Doing the documentation first is a powerful design tool. It ferrets out the nebulous ideas and clarifies them in the mind of the programmer. The user will never be able to read your thoughts or sketchy notes as you begin a project, but he will surely read your preliminary user manual. If you do the documentation first, you will put the user first. In so doing, you will expose the details of the program for yourself. Oddly enough, doing the documentation first is more fun because, as the project proceeds, delaying documentation compounds the difficulty and it becomes a chore.

On major programming projects, the better ones, good documentation is identified by several characteristics:

1. *Readability is the major goal.* Documentation is meant to be read by other human beings. With proper documentation, the reader does not have to stare at a shelf of material with no idea of where to begin.

2. *Documentation is considered important.* The what, when, and how of good documentation are recorded somewhere (i.e., standardized), and help is available to understand the standards.

3. *The required documentation is planned from the beginning.* Some documents are written long before others and serve as guides for the later ones.

4. *Documentation is part of the daily programming process.* Finger paralyzing treatises on long-forgotten topics are not needed. The documentation system drives the programming process!

5. *There is no pressure to skimp.* Someone asks for needed documentation, someone else reads it, and the end reward is the production of high-quality documentation.

In all honesty, documentation is rarely as good as all this. It is possible to be involved in a programming project with a less than perfect documentation system. The point is that, in this event, it is incumbent upon you to develop your own ideas and procedures early.

We all should be able to recognize good documentation. The only thing left to do is to begin providing it. While you may not achieve good documentation right away, any step in that direction is to be preferred to the confusion that will result if you delay documentation later in the project. Try it once. You will see the point.

Proverb 5   **THINK FIRST, CODE LATER**   *Man is obviously made to think.*
PASCAL

There is as much literature on the mechanics of the golf swing as there is on the mechanics of programming. Without exception, professional golfers have mastered the mechanics of the golf swing. But there is more. In a recent televised tournament, one such professional golfer was leading by two strokes going into the final hole. He placed his tee shot into a fairway bunker, tried to reach the green and hit a greenside bunker, bladed the next shot into a bunker on the other side of the green, pitched onto the green, two-putted for a six that tied the tournament, and then lost it on the first play-off hole. The television commentator asked in effect: "Why didn't he think? All he had to do was lay up out of the first bunker, pitch it on the green and two-putt for a five. He just didn't think!"

In much the same way, the mechanics of programming, relative to thinking about the problems of programming, can be mastered without undue difficulty. This proverb is intimately connected with the previous proverbs; the difference is that once the mechanical procedures of problem definition and documentation are finished, the essential task is to start thinking about the solution as soon as possible.

The proverb is literal: Think first means think—do not code! Start thinking while the problem is fresh in your mind and the deadline is as far away as it will ever be. Consider at least two different ways to solve the problem. Examine the approaches to discover possible trouble spots or areas where the solution appears difficult. Our professional golfer should have thought: the only way I can lose this tournament is to hit the ball into that greenside bunker. You should think that the only way this program will crash is if there is a faulty algorithm.

Code later means giving yourself time to weed out the difficult parts and polishing the algorithm before trying to formalize it in actual code. It is easier to clarify thoughts now than to discard poor programs later.

This proverb is most often violated by a "linear" approach to programming. This simply means that a programmer receives a problem and immediately starts preparing the code to solve it. Tempting as this approach may be, avoid it for it is full of hidden costs and dangers. Without thinking first, you may be coding for an ill-conceived program or—the ultimate foolishness—writing a program that you will have to throw away later.

In conclusion, remember Murphy's second law of programming: "it always takes longer to write a program than you think." A corollary might be: the sooner you start coding the program instead of thinking about it, the longer it will take to finish it.

| Proverb 6 | ***PROCEED TOP-DOWN*** | *The last thing one settles in writing a book is what one puts in first.*
 PASCAL |

A major objective of this book is to advocate the "top-down" approach to programming problems. The top-down approach is itself subject to several interpretations, but many of these overlook important issues. Top-down programming is discussed at length in Chapter 5; however, following these rules of the top-down approach is the essence of this proverb:

1. Design the top levels first.

2. Use language-independent forms initially.

3. Postpone details to lower levels.

4. Formalize each level.

5. Verify each level.

6. Make successive refinements.

Consider the example in Figure 1-3. Here is the first pass at the top level for the programming problem of Chapter 7. Examining the definition of the problem, the programmer writes an informal program, P1 (first pass) in pseudocode. After a more detailed look at the problem definition and considering the overall algorithm, the programmer develops P1 into a more refined version, P2 (second pass). The main program ultimately emerges and can be verified by testing. The code to produce the modules referenced in the final pass at the program must be developed in P2 and further refined in successive levels.

Top-down programming has two distinct advantages. First, a programmer is freed from the confines of a particular language and can deal with the more natural data structure of the program. Second, top-down programming leads to a modular approach that allows the programmer to write statements relevant to that program structure. The details can be developed later in separate modules. The main goal of top-down programming is to aid the programmer in writing well-structured, modular programs.

The substance of this proverb will be amplified in Chapter 7. For now, Pascal's observation means this for the top-down approach: One does not write the first lines of the program first. One designs and writes the main control routine, the "top" level, first.

Figure 1-3.   ***Initial stages of program development***

P1 (First pass)

```
initialize program variables
welcome players
do
   get a proposed move
   if move is legal then
      process the move
   if the game is not over then
      change players
   else
      exit
while not game over
```

P2 (Second pass)

```
initialize (PLAYER, BOARD)
write (INTRODUCTORY_MESSAGES)

do
   get (MOVE) from PLAYER
   if LEGAL_MOVE (PLAYER, BOARD, MOVE) then
      UPDATE_BOARD (PLAYER, BOARD, MOVE)
      if LEGAL_JUMP (PLAYER, BOARD, MOVE)
      and JUMP_CAN_BE_CONTINUED (PLAYER, BOARD, MOVE) then
         CONTINUE_THE_JUMP (PLAYER, BOARD, MOVE)
      if NO_KING (BOARD, PLAYER)
      and MOVES_LEFT (BOARD, OPPONENT) then
        swap PLAYERS
        prompt OPPONENT for next MOVE
      else
        write (WINNING_MSG) for PLAYER
        write (LOSING_MSG) for OPPONENT
        GAME_OVER is true
      else
        write (ILLEGAL_MOVE_MSG) for PLAYER
while not GAME_OVER
```

Proverb 7

BEWARE OF OTHER APPROACHES

Beware of false prophets, which come to you in sheep's clothing, but inwardly are ravening wolves.
Matthew, VII: 12

Programmers have traditionally used many different approaches to programming. Consider the following:

1. Bottom-up approach.

2. Inside-out approach.

3. Linear approach.

4. Typical systems analyst approach.

5. Imitation approach.

Bottom-Up Approach

In the "bottom-up" approach, the programmer writes the lower modules first and the upper levels later. This bottom-up approach is an inversion of the top-down approach. Its weakness lies in enticing the programmer to make specific decisions about the program before the overall problem and algorithm are understood.

Inside-Out Approach

There are four other approaches to programming between the bottom-up and top-down. The "inside-out" or "forest" approach means, simply, starting in the middle of the program and working down and up at the same time. As such a method is convenient, it is therefore popular and needs closer examination. Roughly speaking, if we followed this approach, we would proceed as follows:

1. *General idea*. First we decide upon the general idea for programming the problem.

2. *A rough sketch of the program*. Next we write any sections of the program that we deem to be "important," assuming

initialization in some form. In some sections we would write portions of the actual code.

3. *Coding the first version.* After Step 2, we write specific codes for the entire program. After one module has been coded, we debug it, and immediately prepare a description of what it does.

4. *Rethinking and revising.* As a result of Step 3, we should be close to a working program, but it may be possible to improve it. So we continue by making several improvements until we obtain a complete working program.

It is fair to say that many programmers work inside-out. Usually, they don't start very close to the top or the bottom of the program. Instead, they begin in the middle and work outward until a program finally emerges. This approach is obviously weak because as programs undergo patches and changes, there is no clear, logical structure for a programmer to follow.

Linear Approach

The third method is the "linear" approach that we introduced in Proverb 5. Here, one starts writing code as it will appear when executed: first line first, second line second, and so forth. This results in making specific detailed decisions with little assurance that they are appropriate to the problem at hand. As poor as this technique may appear to be, there is a strong temptation to employ it, especially on "easy" programs. But be particularly wary of this temptation: there is no such thing as an "easy" program.

Systems-Analyst Approach

The fourth technique is the typical "systems-analyst" approach. When used wisely, it can be an effective technique, and admittedly it has been successfully used for many large programs. We shall briefly compare it with the top-down approach, the technique advocated in this book.

The systems analyst often starts on a large programming problem by dividing up the task on the basis of the flow of control he sees in the overall program. The program is broken into a number of modules, which are then farmed out to the programmers. After these have been completed, the analyst will firm up the interfaces and try to make things work right. The lower-level modules receive special attention since their function and data handling are used often.

With the top-down approach, on the other hand, the flow of control is subservient to the logical structure. There does not have to be an identifiable flow of control that is easy to flowchart. The flow of control is rather like traversing a tree. It starts at the top level, goes down one or more levels, comes back, goes on to another level, and so forth. The top-down approach thus has little need for flowcharting.

Imitation Approach

As a final method, consider what I call the "imitation" approach, a method superficially resembling the top-down approach. This approach is discussed in detail because many programmers *think* that the top-down approach is really the way they have always programmed. The imitation approach is described as follows:

1. *Thinking about the program.* Having been given a programming assignment, take the time to examine the problem thoroughly before starting to program. Think about the details of the program for a while, and then decide on a general approach.

2. *Deciding on submodules.* After having thought about the problem in detail, decide on what sections will be sufficiently important to merit being made into submodules.

3. *Data representation.* After compiling a list of the submodules, decide on a data representation that will enable them to be efficient, unless the representation is already specified.

4. *Coding of submodules.* At this point, write each submodule. After each is completed, write down what it expects as input, what it returns as output, and what it does. The submodules should be written in a hierarchical manner: the most primitive first, calling routines second,

and so forth. Doing this will ensure that the submodules are fully coded before the upper-level program structures are finalized.

5. *Coding the main program.* After all submodules have been written, write the main program. The purpose of the main program will be sequencing and interfacing the subroutines.

The imitation approach has some important resemblances to the top-down approach:

1. The programmer must understand the problem thoroughly before writing code.

2. The actual writing of the program is postponed until after certain decisions have been made.

3. The problem is broken up into logical units.

However, there are important different characteristics in the two approaches.

Top-Down Approach

1. In the top-down approach, a specific plan of attack is developed in stages. Only the issues relevant to a given level are considered, and these issues are formalized completely.

2. Furthermore, whenever the programmer decides to use a subprogram, the interfaces (i.e., arguments, returned values, and effects) are decided first. The inputs and outputs are formalized before developing the submodule; that is, the submodules are made to fit the calling routine instead of the other way around.

3. Most important, at every step in the top-down approach, the programmer has a complete, correct "program."

The major disadvantages of the imitation approach are that it is more likely to produce errors, usually requires major program modifications, or results in a somewhat ill-conceived program. Choosing a partially specified attack may require serious changes to the program. Coding submodules first may result in a confusing program logic, if the submodules do not happen to integrate easily into the upper-level code designed later.

In summary, think carefully about programming technique. The top-down approach, which is discussed at length in Chapter 5, is the smart alternative.

2 *STRUCTURE IS LOGIC*

Rose is a rose is a rose is a rose.

> Gertrude Stein
> *Sacred Emily*

An idealist is one who, on noticing that a rose smells better than a cabbage, concludes that it will also make better soup.

> H. L. Mencken
> *Sententiae*

Proverb 8 | ***CODE IT FOR THE OTHER GUY*** | *Our life is frittered away by detail . . . Simplify, simplify.*
HENRY DAVID THOREAU
Walden: Where I lived, and what I lived for

Have you ever put together one of those "easily assembled" toys on Christmas eve? The instructions read:

Attach the tower(B) to the base(A) and the chute(C) to the tower.

In the same manner, the next page of instructions directs:

The kit contains 16 3/4″ bolts. Insert each one into the holes marked "J"; place base(A) snugly so edges(L) are aligned with arrows *inside* base(A). In kit 2, take nuts(D) and . . .

and so on, etc. You wonder if the designer of the toy was ever in communication with the author of the instructions on how to put the toy together.

In programming, we have the same problem. Somehow, we get so caught up in design that we forget the user, we forget to code it for the other guy. Eventually, programs work, but that is not the test of a good program. The test is: can a program be easily understood, are there no unnecessary details, and is the logical structure clear? Well-structured programs are the mark of a careful development process and are usually characterized by small, functionally specific modules. Generally, the statements of a C module should not extend beyond one page.

Just like the instructions for assembling the toy, some programmers write calls to procedures like this:

```
READ_TABLE;
PROCESS_TRANSACTION;
UPDATE_STATUS;
```

and then you turn to this:

```
UPDATE_STATUS ()
    /* Update data base file with new information */
{
    fscanf (file_1, "%c", &CONTROL)
    TRANS.COUNT    = 0;
    TRANS.ON       = 0;
    TRANS.BUFFSIZE = 100;

  if (FIELD.INDICATOR != TERM_VAL)
     . . .
    while (STATE_VAR = GO_VAL) {
        HANDLE(NEW_TRANS, COUNTER, @RESULT_STATUS);
        UPDATE_TRANSFILE;
        ++ACOUNT;
        . . .

    }
    . . .

}
```

If you throw your hands up with this, it is understandable. Someone seems to be lying. Why? In this case:

1. The function UPDATE_STATUS has probably ten(!) purposes.

2. There may be fifteen or so effective inputs or outputs, each buried in the code.

We need to answer the question: What is a logical structure, and what is a logical unit? It is a section of code, normally a function or procedure with:

    1. a *single* purpose, and

    2. clearly stated inputs and outputs.

Programmers usually violate these two points, and getting to the bottom of such matters is, in a sense, the thrust of this book.

    The most direct value of modular code is felt during program maintenance, for time is not wasted trying to determine what is being done over several sections of code. Consider Figure 2-1A, which outlines the logical structure of a hypothetical program. The structure is difficult to follow. Figure 2-1B pictures the remedied situation where simple computations are isolated into units.

Figure 2-1.   ***Display of logical structure***

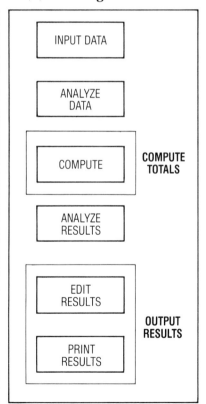

(A) Poor logical structure   *(B) Better logical structure*

There are many advantages to modular code. Coding time is shortened by the use of previously written modules. Implementation costs are lower because of easier changes, decreased re-compilation costs, smaller tasks, and isolated code bottlenecks. Testing is simpler because "simple" modules usually have not more than, say, a half dozen looping and branching constructs and thus a smaller number of total execution paths. In the end, the dividend is paid in the maintenance of the program.

When the time comes to write the actual code, there are three guidelines that will help you code in logical units:

1. First, and most obviously, make the best use subprograms.

2. Avoid confusing control structures.

3. Display the resulting logical structure with good spacing and indentation.

The next three proverbs treat these issues. But if you think of yourself as the other guy, and simplify, simplify, both the process and the product will be improved.

Proverb 9   **MAKE FILES INTO PACKAGES**

When I was a ten-year-old girl, my uncle gave me a little Russian doll that looked like an Easter egg. If you turned the head, the egg-doll opened and inside there was another doll until at last, opening the smallest doll, I found a piece of chocolate. But after I had put the dolls back together again, there was no chocolate at the end of my search. I did not understand this, although I tried again and again to find the chocolate.
ANONYMOUS

A C program consists of:

- a sequence of files, one of which contains the main program routine.

The main program is a function called MAIN. So far, so good. A file consists of:

- a sequence of declarative items.

A declarative item can be a function definition, variable declaration, or any declaration for that matter. So far, still so good.
Now for the big point:

- The best model for the contents of a file is the concept of a "package."

What does this mean? Let's try.
We are familiar with the idea of a library package of mathematical routines. This might be a file like

```
/* -- File math.c
   -- general declarations */

float sin(x)
    definition
}

float cos(x)
    definition
}
. . .
```

The file will probably include definitions of sin, cos, tan, arctan, log, and so forth. This is a model package.

- A package is a group of items (functions, types, constants, and variables) related to a single purpose.

In the simplest case, a package can be a collection of constants, for instance

```
/* File plot.h */
float X_MIN, Y_MIN  = 0.0;
float X_MAX, Y_MAX  = 100.0;
float DELTA         = 0.1;
float MISSING_VALUE = 1.0;
```

In a more complex example, a program will consist of a number of files, each of which should capture knowledge of one concept. Imagine a program to monitor a game of checkers. Two users input moves for playing a game, and the program displays the board and enforces the rules. Such a program can be organized in endless ways, but one good way is shown in Figure 2-2.

Figure 2-2.   *Use of Packages*

```
/* -- Main program file, checkers.c
      -- General comments describing the overall program
      -- and its design */


#include "general.h"
#include "board.h"
#include "user.h"


main (argc, argv)
int argc;
char *argv [];
{
      ...
      color PLAYER, OPPONENT;
      ...
      SET_UP (BOARD);
      ...
      -- main algorithm
      ...
}
-------------------------------


/* -- Header file board.h
   -- Constants, types, and functions for the BOARD */

#define NUM_SQS 32

typedef enum {BLACK, RED} color;
typedef enum {BLACK_PIECE, RED_PIECE, VACANT} sq_status;
...
extern boolean JUMP_AVAILABLE (/* PLAYER, BOARD */);
...
-------------------------------
```

```
/* -- Computation file board.c
   -- Support functions for operating on the BOARD */

#include "general.h"
#include "board.h"


...


boolean JUMP_AVAILABLE (PLAYER, BOARD)
     board_contents BOARD;
     color PLAYER;
     ...
}
...
---------------------------------

/* -- Header File user.h
   -- User interface input and output */

#define MAX_LINE_SIZE 72;
...
typedef char input_buffer [MAX_LINE_SIZE];
...
extern SEND_MSG (/* PLAYER, MSG_ID */);
...
--------------------------------

/* File user.c */

#include "general.h"
#include <stdio.h>
#include "user.h"
...
SEND_MSG (PLAYER, MSG_ID)
     color PLAYER;
     msg_name MSG_ID;
     ...
}


GET_LINE (PLAYER, BUFFER)
     color PLAYER;
     input_buffer BUFFER;
     ...
}
...
```

```
----------------------------------

/* -- Header file general.h
   -- General language constants */

#define FALSE 0
#define TRUE  1
#define boolean short
...
```

Consider the file "board". This file contains only declarations. The declarations define the organization of the checker board, the legal adjacent squares, and the headers for several external functions. These functions check if a jump is available, if a move is legal, and so on. This and the other files reflect these concepts:

checkers.c	The main program.
board.h.	Definitions for using the board.
board.c	Code for the functions specified in board.h.
user.h	Definitions for user i/o.
user.c	Code for functions specified in user.h.
general.h	Generally useful constants.

These support files are used by the main routines, given in the file checkers.c.

I do not wish to imply that getting a good overall package design is easy. It is not. But the physical concept of a file is an ideal match for the logical concept of a package.

Moral: A file is not just a place to hold some code. Rather, we should think:

1 file ◄──► 1 package ◄──► 1 purpose

The file is the cornerstone of good program structure.

Proverb 10 ***BLACK-BOX YOUR***
SUBROUTINES

*Years later, when I was older and
my uncle was in the evening of his
life, he came to visit and asked
about the egg-doll that he had given
me. When I brought it to him, I
found that the smallest doll had
been broken. I was sad. "Do not cry,
my child," he said. "But I cannot
replace the smallest doll, only the
whole doll. Some times, one must
replace the whole to repair the
part."*
ANONYMOUS

The function facilities in C are a powerful tool for coding clear,
modular programs. Not only do these facilities allow the programmer to "factor out" sections of code, but more importantly,
they provide a basic unit for abstraction of program modules.
This abstraction can have a great effect on program readability
by exposing the program's logical structure, *even if* the function
is called only once.

Most languages (but not C) make a distinction between:

(**a**) a subprogram that returns a value and thus acts as an
expression.

(**b**) a subprogram that does not return a value and acts as a
statement.

In Pascal, Modula-2, and Ada, these two subprograms are called:

(**a**) a function.

(**b**) a procedure.

In C, the only ready analog is:

(**a**) a function.

(**b**) a "void" or "statement" function.

but this is more tongue-twisting than helpful. Hence, we will oc-
casionally use the term "procedure" when we refer to a void
function.

35

The basic idea behind functions is an old and familiar one. We almost grow up with the little mapping

$$F(X, Y) \rightarrow Z$$

which can also be expressed as

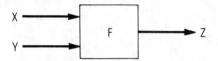

This latter view suggests that F is some algorithm expressed in a programming language. Fine, so far.

But when the going gets rough, programmers lose this simple idea. A procedure or function should have all its inputs and outputs identified. Even something like a procedure to update an array should follow the rule. For instance, consider the array BOARD in

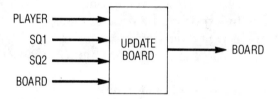

This can be expressed by the procedure header

```
UPDATE_BOARD (/* for */ PLAYER,
              /* using */ SQ1, SQ2,
              /* updating */ BOARD)
```

This is the *full* interface for this procedure, no matter how complex its internal algorithm.

Consider the programs of Figure 2-3. Given the values for the three-element arrays A, B, C, and D, the programs use the determinant method (assuming DENOM is nonzero) to solve three independent equations of the following form for the unknowns x, y, and z:

$$A_1x + B_1y + C_1z = D_1$$
$$A_2x + B_2y + C_2z = D_2$$
$$A_3x + B_3y + D_3z = D_3$$

The program of Figure 2-3A is a confusion of arithmetic calculations. It contains little hint of the determinant method or the algorithm needed to solve the problem. In contrast, Figure 2-3B uses a function subprogram to calculate the determinants. It is explicitly clear that each unknown is the quotient of two determinants and that the denominator is the determinant of the variable coefficient matrix. Figure 2-3C shows an even greater improvement when the arrays are passed as arguments.

There are two points of Figure 2-3C: first, by black-boxing subroutines, the entire structure of the program is more logical; second, your program will be longer. But in this fashion, you can use functions and procedures *often*. The other guy can read it more easily, and maintenance and debugging are easier when we can, as with the doll, replace the entire black box rather than tamper with the individual parts.

Figure 2-3. *Solution of three independent equations*

(A) Poor solution: functions not used

```
/* program EQUATION_1 */
#include <stdio.h>
#define NUM_UNKNOWNS 3


main ()
{

    typedef float coefficients [NUM_UNKNOWNS + 1];
    coefficients A, B, C, D;
    float DENOM;
    float X, Y, Z;
    short I;

    printf ("Enter coefficients: \n");
    for (I = 1; I <= NUM_UNKNOWNS; ++I)
        scanf ("%f %f %f %f", &A[I], &B[I], &C[I], &D[I]);

    DENOM =  (A[1]*B[2]*C[3]) + (A[2]*B[3]*C[1]) + (A[3]*B[1]*C[2])
          -  (A[3]*B[2]*C[1]) - (A[2]*B[1]*C[3]) - (A[1]*B[3]*C[2]);

    X =  (D[1]*B[2]*C[3]) + (D[2]*B[3]*C[1]) + (D[3]*B[1]*C[2])
      -  (D[3]*B[2]*C[1]) - (D[2]*B[1]*C[3]) - (D[1]*B[3]*C[2]);
```

```
    Y =  (A[1]*D[2]*C[3]) + (A[2]*D[3]*C[1]) + (A[3]*D[1]*C[2])
      -  (A[3]*D[2]*C[1]) - (A[2]*D[1]*C[3]) - (A[1]*D[3]*C[2]);

    Z =  (A[1]*B[2]*D[3]) + (A[2]*B[3]*D[1]) + (A[3]*B[1]*D[2])
      -  (A[3]*B[2]*D[1]) - (A[2]*B[1]*D[3]) - (A[1]*B[3]*D[2]);

    X = X / DENOM;
    Y = Y / DENOM;
    Z = Z / DENOM;
    printf ("Unknowns are: %g, %g, %g\n", X, Y, Z);
}
```

(B) Better solution: a function used

```
/* program EQUATION_2 */

#include <stdio.h>
#define NUM_UNKNOWNS 3

float DETERM (X1,X2,X3, Y1,Y2,Y3, Z1,Z2,Z3)
    float X1, X2, X3,
          Y1, Y2, Y3,
          Z1, Z2, Z3;
{
    float RESULT;

    RESULT =  (X1*Y2*Z3) + (X2*Y3*Z1) + (X3*Y1*Z2)
           -  (X3*Y2*Z1) - (X2*Y1*Z3) - (X1*Y3*Z2);
    return (RESULT);
}


main ()
{

    typedef float coefficients [NUM_UNKNOWNS + 1];
    coefficients A, B, C, D;
    float DENOM;
    float X, Y, Z;
    short I;

    printf ("Enter coefficients: \n");

    for (I = 1; I <= NUM_UNKNOWNS; ++I)
        scanf ("%f %f %f %f", &A[I], &B[I], &C[I], &D[I]);
```

```
    DENOM =  DETERM (A[1], B[1], C[1], A[2], B[2], C[2], A[3], B[3], C[3]);


    X =  DETERM (D[1], B[1], C[1], D[2], B[2], C[2], D[3], B[3], C[3]);
    Y =  DETERM (A[1], D[1], C[1], A[2], D[2], C[2], A[3], D[3], C[3]);
    Z =  DETERM (A[1], B[1], D[1], A[2], B[2], D[2], A[3], B[3], D[3]);

    X = X / DENOM;
    Y = Y / DENOM;
    Z = Z / DENOM;
    printf ("Unknowns are: %g, %g, %g\n", X, Y, Z);

}
```

(C) Still better solution: using a function and passing arrays

```
/* program EQUATION_3 */

#include <stdio.h>
#define NUM_UNKNOWNS 3

typedef float coefficients [NUM_UNKNOWNS + 1];

float DETERM(R, S, T)
    coefficients R, S, T;
{
    float RESULT;

    RESULT =  (R[1]*S[2]*T[3]) + (R[2]*S[3]*T[1]) + (R[3]*S[1]*T[2])
            - (R[3]*S[2]*T[1]) - (R[2]*S[1]*T[3]) - (R[1]*S[3]*T[2]);
    return (RESULT);
}

main ()
{
    coefficients A, B, C, D;
    float DENOM;
    float X, Y, Z;
    short I;
    printf ("Enter coefficients: \n");
    for (I = 1; I <= NUM_UNKNOWNS; ++I)
        scanf ("%f %f %f %f", &A[I], &B[I], &C[I], &D[I]);

    DENOM = DETERM(A, B, C);
```

```
X = DETERM(D, B, C) / DENOM;
Y = DETERM(A, D, C) / DENOM;
Z = DETERM(A, B, D) / DENOM;
printf ("Unknowns are: %g, %g, %g\n", X, Y, Z);
}
```

Proverb 11   *DON'T GOTO*

> *A little neglect may breed mischief . . . for want of a nail, the shoe was lost; for want of a shoe, the horse was lost; for want of a horse, the rider was lost.*
>
> BENJAMIN FRANKLIN
> *Maxims, prefixed to Poor Richard's Almanack*

Earlier we observed that program documentation was a controversial issue in programming. But even more controversy has been generated over control structures. What is the best way to ensure that at every point in a program the next action to be carried out will be clearly specified? In many languages, the control structure issue focuses on one small statement: the goto.

The unconditional transfer of control, which is the purpose of the goto statement, has been associated with programming since its inception. Its historical ties have left indelible marks on today's major programming languages. Until recently, virtually all higher-level languages have had some form of an unrestricted goto. My position is this: make a little sign and hang it where you can see it every day:

DO NOT GOTO

YOU DON'T HAVE TO

Let me show you why. Consider the following little example.

```
    SUM   = 0;
    COUNT = 0;

L1: if (COUNT > MAX)
        goto L2;
    SUM   += COUNT;
    COUNT += 2;
```

```
     goto L1;
L2: printf ("%d\n", SUM);
```

This is hardly complex, but does make the point. The goto's force us to develop a mental image of chasing about. This disappears with the alternative rendering:

```
SUM   = 0;
COUNT = 0;
while (COUNT <= MAX) {
     SUM   += COUNT;
     COUNT += 2;
}
printf ("%d\n", SUM);
```

Moreover, it is now really clear that the program contains a single loop, and when the loop is complete, COUNT is greater than MAX.

In another setting, consider the two programs of Figure 2-4. Here we see simple subroutines for extracting of a substring (designated by two character positions) in a given source string. Under certain conditions, the subroutine sets an error flag.

In particular, both segments of code perform the following computation.

Inputs:

SOURCE__STR:	a string of characters
STR__LENGTH:	the length of the string
POS1, POS2:	the start and end positions of a substring

Outputs:

SUB__STR:	the substring of SOURCE__STR from POS1 to POS2
ERROR:	FALSE if (POS1 <= POS2) and (0 <= POS1) and (POS2 <= 100) TRUE otherwise

Here the type

```
typedef char STRING[101];
```

is assumed. Also, if ERROR is true, no value is assigned to SUB__STR.

41

In Figure 2-4A, we see a quite tightly nested series of interconnected if statements. In Figure 2-4B, we have a program derived from the use of alternative control structures. The second example provides a much clearer description of the algorithm, mainly because of the use of simple 1-in, 1-out control structures.

Figure 2-4.   *Control structures*

(A) Poor

```
        if (POS1 < 0)
            goto L1;
        else
            goto L2;
L1:     ERROR = TRUE;
        goto L5;
L2:     if ((POS2 < POS1) || (POS2 > 100))
            goto L1;
        else
            goto L3;
L3:     if ((POS2 - POS1) > LENGTH)
            goto L1;
        else
            goto L4;
L4:     ERROR = FALSE;
        for (I = POS1; I <= POS2; ++I) {
            CHAR_POS = (I - POS1);
            SUB_STR[CHAR_POS] = SOURCE_STR[I];
        }
L5:     /* done */;
```

(B) Better

```
if ((POS1 < 0) || (POS2 < POS1) || (POS2 > 100)
|| (POS2 - POS1 > LENGTH))
    ERROR = TRUE;
else {
    ERROR = FALSE;
    for (I = POS1; I <= POS2; ++I) {
        CHAR_POS = (I - POS1);
        SUB_STR[CHAR_POS] = SOURCE_STR[I];
    }
}
```

The differences between these two programs are quite clearly expressed in their corresponding flowcharts, shown in Figures 2-5 and 2-6. In the first illustration, the flowchart shows a profusion of branching lines; in the second, a clearer structure is evident.

Figure 2-5.   **Flowchart for Figure 2-4A**

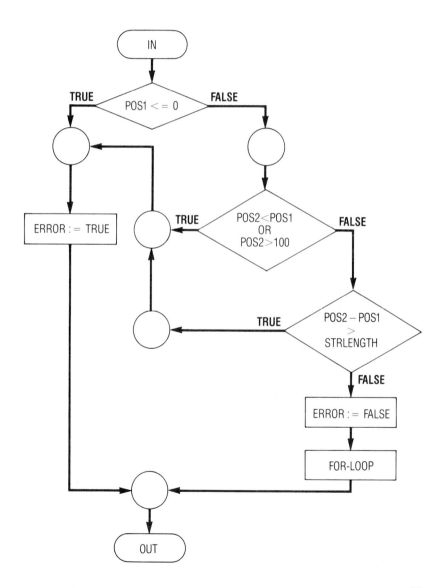

In yet another setting, consider the program segments of Figure 2-7. These segments employ a variation of the bubble sort algorithm to sort an array A, containing 10 entries. The array A is declared of type

```
typedef float A[NUM_ELEMENTS];
```

Figure 2-6.   ***Flowchart for Figure 2-4B***

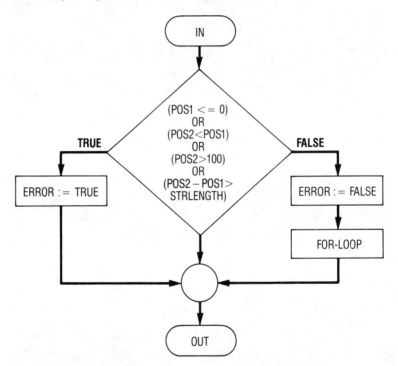

The subroutine SWAP exchanges the values of the two variables given as arguments. Basically, the programs scan the array A once from the bottom (position 0) to the top (position 9). At each examined position in the array, the elements at the top of the position are already in order, and the program checks to see if the element in the next position is itself in order. If not, the element is swapped with the previous element and then "bubbled"

Figure 2-7.   *A variant of the bubble sort algorithm*

(A) Poor

```
#define NUM_ELEMENTS 10
int I, J;
float A[NUM_ELEMENTS];

{
     I = NUM_ELEMENTS - 1;
L1: if (I == 0)
        goto L5;
     J = 0;

L2: if (J == I)
        goto L4;
     if (A[J] <= A[J+1])
        goto L3;
     SWAP (&A[J], &A[J+1]);

L3: ++J;
     goto L2;

L4: I = I - 1;
     goto L1;

L5: for (I = 0; I < NUM_ELEMENTS; ++I)
        printf ("%f\n", A[I]);

}
```

(B) Better

```
#define NUM_ELEMENTS 10
int I, J;
float A[NUM_ELEMENTS];

{
     for (I = NUM_ELEMENTS; I >= 1; --I) {
         for (J = 0; J < (I - 1); ++J)
             if (A[J] > A[J+1])
                 SWAP (&A[J], &A[J+1]);
     }
     for (I = 0; I < NUM_ELEMENTS; ++I)
         printf ("%f\n", A[I]);
}
```

up until its proper place in the sorted part of the array is found. Processing then continues at the position below the element originally examined.

One point of this example is that the (possibly) small gain in efficiency via the goto is not as important as the improvement in clarity when the programmer uses alternative ways of constructing his program.

The trap that programmers fall into is trying to "get rid" of goto's. If you play that game, the secret to winning is to start from the problem. Someone says, "Hey, this goto is perfect."

```
while (I < J) {
        . . .
        if (X < Y) {
                . . .
                goto L99;
                . . .
        }
        . . .
    }
    . . .
L99: DOSOMETHING;
```

You are at a loss. But, just start over from the problem. Try to undo the logic that led to this deeply embedded goto. The name of the real game is to *program without* goto's. The reason is to *force* a clear, sensible logic to all your code.

In summary, the deeper issue here is not merely the elimination of goto's but the use of a clear, logical program structure. The trouble with goto's is that when they are abused, they can lead a programmer down the path of a confusing, almost spaghettilike, logic. Chapter 5, which discusses program standards, provides specific rules for the use of well-formed control structures. If you stick to these standards *from the beginning*, the goto problem may go away.

As in all four proverbs of this section, the deeper issue here is not the elimination of goto's, nesting, or black-boxing—it is coding in logical structure so the other guy can read it.

3 *CODING THE PROGRAM*

Works done least rapidly, art most cherishes.

Robert Browning
Old pictures in Florence, Stanza 17

Proverb 12 | ***ALL WORDS MEAN SOMETHING*** | *"When I use a word," Humpty Dumpty said, in a rather scornful tone, "it means just what I choose it to mean - neither more nor less." "The question is," Alice said, "whether you can make words mean so many different things."*
LEWIS CARROLL
Alice Through the Looking Glass

The adjective "mnemonic" is a useful modifier for programmers, since precision in choosing words is necessary. It means ". . .assisting or intending to assist the memory." As it is difficult to overestimate the value of using mnemonic, user-defined names, it is also easy to become careless using names that may later complicate or confuse the intent of a program. Principles for selecting good mnemonic names are discussed at length in Chapter 6. Here it is sufficient to make one point: use names that correctly reflect the objects they are intended to represent.

The disadvantage of poor names is easily seen in Figure 3-1. The programmer who writes code like the code shown in Figure 3-1A will probably need to keep a separate list specifying what each variable name represents. Otherwise, the programmer may lose track of what each variable does. Figure 3-1B significantly clarifies the situation. The names themselves almost state the intended calculation.

Figure 3-1B, however, is written using variable names with a maximum length of six characters (the requirement in standard FORTRAN). Figure 3-1C shows the possibilities in Pascal, and Figure 3-1D illustrates the possibilities in languages like C and Ada that allow break characters within names. Certainly OVER-TIMEWAGE and OVERTIME__WAGE are more informative than OVTIME.

Figure 3-1.   **Use of mnemonic names**

(A) Poor (BASIC revisited)

```
LET G = (W * H) + (O * X)
LET T = Rl * G
LET S = Sl * G
LET P = G - T - S
```

(B) Better (FORTRAN revisited)

```
GROSS = (WAGE * HOURS) + (OVTIME * XHOURS)
TAX   = TAXRATE * GROSS
SSEC  = SSRATE * GROSS
PAY   = GROSS - TAX - SSEC
```

(C) Best (good use of Pascal)

```
GROSSPAY    := (WAGE * HOURS) + (OVERTIMEWAGE * EXTRAHOURS);
TAX         := TAXRATE * GROSSPAY;
SOCSECURITY := SOCSECRATE * GROSSPAY;
NETPAY      := GROSSPAY - TAX - SOCSECURITY;
```

(D) Best (the C option)

```
GROSS_PAY     = (WAGE * HOURS) + (OVERTIME_WAGE * EXTRA_HOURS);
TAX           = TAX_RATE * GROSS_PAY;
SOC_SECURITY  = SOC_SEC_RATE * GROSS_PAY;
NET_PAY       = GROSS_PAY - TAX - SOC_SECURITY;
```

The challenge in picking names is somehow to balance the following criteria:

a. accuracy

b. brevity

c. spurious effects.

For instance, consider Figure 3-2A. The names here might appear fine at first glance. But look at these problems.

SUIT__NUM	it is not a variable, as suggested by the name.
D	too short for a major name.
INDEX	too long for an innocent count? Yes or No?
COUNTS	the plural is odd.
R__VAL	cryptic.

These problems are rectified in Figure 3-2B.

Figure 3-2.   *Use of mnemonic names*

(A) Paying token homage

```
#define SUIT_NUM  4
#define RANK_NUM 13
#define CARD_NUM 51
#define DECK_NUM 52

typedef struct {
    int S_VAL;
    int R_VAL;
} card;

typedef char name[6];
typedef int  rank[RANK_NUM+1];
typedef card deck[DECK_NUM];

PRINT_CARD (D)
    deck D;

    /* -- This procedure examines a deck of cards with one missing
       -- card. It finds and prints the rank (e.g., "THREE" or
       -- "KING") of the missing card. */
{
```

```
        rank  COUNTS;
        name  NAME_STR;
        int   RANK_VAL;
        int   INDEX;

        for   (RANK_VAL = 1; RANK_VAL <= RANK_NUM; ++RANK_VAL)
              COUNTS[RANK_VAL] = 0;

        for   (INDEX = 0; INDEX < CARD_NUM; ++INDEX) {
              RANK_VAL = D[INDEX].R_VAL;
              ++COUNTS[RANK_VAL];
        }

        for   (RANK_VAL = 1; RANK_VAL <= RANK_NUM; ++RANK_VAL)
              if (COUNTS[RANK_VAL] < SUIT_NUM)
                  NAME_STR = RANK_NAME[RANK_VAL];

        printf ("Missing rank: %s\n", NAME_STR);
}
```

(B) More accurate names

```
#define NUM_SUITS   4
#define NUM_RANKS   13
#define NUM_CARDS   51
#define DECK_SIZE   52

typedef struct {
      int SUIT_VAL;
      int RANK_VAL;
} card_info;

typedef char      rank_name[6];
typedef int       rank_tally[NUM_RANKS + 1];
typedef card_info deck_contents[DECK_SIZE];

FIND_MISSING_CARD (DECK)
      deck_contents DECK;

      /* -- This procedure examines a deck of cards with one missing card.
         -- It finds and prints the rank (e.g., "THREE" or
         -- "KING") of the missing card. */
{
```

```
rank_tally COUNT;
rank_name NAME;
int I, RANK;

for (RANK = 1; RANK <= NUM_RANKS; ++RANK)
     COUNT[RANK] = 0;

for (I = 0; I < NUM_CARDS; ++I) {
     RANK = DECK[I].RANK_VAL;
     ++COUNT[RANK];
}

for (RANK = 1; RANK <= NUM_RANKS; ++RANK)
     if (COUNT[RANK] < NUM_SUITS)
          NAME = RANK_NAME[RANK];

printf ("Missing rank: %s\n", NAME);
}
```

These examples indicate that the thoughtful use of mnemonic names improves the readability for the programmer and for those who read the program later. It is worth the time to devise and use informative names. You may not fully appreciate the benefits of your efforts now, but you will when a large program has to be debugged or modified later. Then you will appreciate that you chose a word to mean exactly what you wanted it to mean. Mnemonic assistance is then priceless.

Proverb 13 ***SPACES HAVE MEANING, TOO***

Well timed silence hath more eloquence than speech.
MARTIN FARQUAHAR TUPPER
Of Discretion

Somewhere, in some graduate student class, a term was coined that may seem trite but, as in the previous proverb, means something: "prettyprinting." Briefly defined, it means the effective use of "extra" spaces, blank lines, or special characters to delineate the logical structure of a program.

Prettyprinting is especially useful in the verification and maintenance of programs. It helps to detect errors, such as improperly structured data description entries and incorrectly nested if statements. Furthermore, a programmer trying to read the program does not have to devote extra time to discovering its structure, an advantage that makes the program considerably easier to understand.

At the "macro" level, the goal of prettyprinting is to show the logical structure of major program units. For instance, suppose we have a program of the form:

a. half page of comments

b. general #define statements

c. half page of declarations

d. a one-page procedure ALPHA

e. a two-page procedure BETA

f. a thirty-line main program.

If this is the structure, then prettyprinting means showing it, not leaving it to the reader to figure it out. The key here is to use breaks between major units. A break can be achieved by (1) a group of 4 or 5 blank lines, (2) a dotted line, or (3) a new page. Figure 3-3 shows one possibility, using dotted lines.

Figure 3-3.   *Displaying overall structure*

```
/* -- program SHOWME
```

-- comments describing
*-- the program */*

```
-------------------------------
```

```
/* -- Definitions */
#define NUM_ITEMS 100
#define MAX_LENGTH 72
...
#define FILE_NAME "entry.dat"
```

```
----------------------------
```

```
/* -- Declarations */
```

type declarations

variable declarations

```
-------------------------------
```

ALPHA *(parameters)*
        parameter declarations
{
        local declarations

        statements
}

```
-------------------------------
```

BETA *(parameters)*
        parameter declarations
{
        local declarations

        statements
}

```
main ()
        declarations
{
        statements for
        main program
}
```

Obvious? Sure, but take a peek at a professional program sometime and see how often it is done.

At the "mini" level, the goal is to show the logical units of a single module. For instance, consider:

```
A_COUNT = 0;
E_COUNT = 0;
I_COUNT = 0;
O_COUNT = 0;
U_COUNT = 0;
while (C != EOF) {
        body of loop
}
```

There *should* be (it is not a matter of "taste") one blank line here. Where? Just before the while loop. Why? Because there are two logical units: (a) initialization of counters, and (b) a processing loop. It is impossible to give hard and fast rules where to put blank lines, but the gist of it is

• between conceptual chunks

Some programmers stuff a few blank lines in just for looks, but the purpose is to show *meaning*.

At the "micro" level, the goal is to show the individual parts of statements. You would be horrified to see

```
A_COUNT       +=    1    ;
```

but not

```
A_COUNT += 1;
```

The reason is that the correct spacing illuminates the correct meaning.

There are all kinds of cases where a little white space is effective. Consider:

```
(a)  A_COUNT=0

(b)  T+R*Q

(c)  printf ("A = %2d",A_COUNT);

(d)  for(I=2;I<=MAX;++I)

(e)  if(HEIGHT<STANDARD). . .

(f)  struct{int X; int Y;} complex

(g)  CARD_VALUE[RANK]+1

(h)  F(X/2.0,Y/2.0,Z/2.0)

(i)  {SUNDAY,MONDAY,TUESDAY}
```

These can all be improved:

```
(a) A_COUNT = 0                  /* shows the two sides */

(b) T + R*Q                      /* shows precedence */

(c) printf ("A= %2d", A_COUNT)   /* shows two arguments */

(d) for (I = 2; I <= MAX; ++I)   /* breathing room */

(e) if (HEIGHT < STANDARD) ...   /* not so crammed */

(f) struct {                     /* really shows it */
        int X;
        int Y;
    } complex

(g) CARD_VALUE[RANK] + 1         /* shows the two sides */

(h) F(X/2.0, Y/2.0, Z/2.0)       /* shows three arguments */

(i) {SUNDAY, MONDAY, TUESDAY}    /* shows three values */
```

Again, the same point

• Meaning, Meaning, Meaning

Yet, professional programmers, students, and authors often miss the point and treat spacing as a second-class issue.

As an example, four complete C programs are listed in Figures 3-4A through 3-4D. The first three are not well prettyprinted; the last shows careful thought in prettyprinting. Even in some textbooks, users of C are seldom exposed to the full potential of prettyprinting, although almost every implementation admits great latitude in the spacing of programs.

Figure 3-4.   ***Prettyprinting***

(A) Lack of prettyprinting

```
/* program VOWELS */
#include <stdio.h>
#define EOL '\n'
main ()
{int A_COUNT, E_COUNT, I_COUNT, O_COUNT, U_COUNT;
char CHARACTER; A_COUNT = 0;
E_COUNT = 0; I_COUNT = 0;
O_COUNT = 0; U_COUNT = 0;
printf("Enter line of text:\n");
do {
scanf ("%c", &CHARACTER);
switch (CHARACTER)
{
case 'A':++A_COUNT;
break;
case 'E':++E_COUNT;
break;
case 'I':++I_COUNT;
break;
case 'O':++O_COUNT;
break;
case 'U':++U_COUNT;
break;
default: /* do nothing */;
}} while (CHARACTER != EOL);
printf(" A = %d   E = %d   I = %d   O = %d   U = %d\n",
A_COUNT, E_COUNT,
I_COUNT, O_COUNT, U_COUNT);
}
```

(B) Giving token thought to prettyprinting

```
/* program VOWELS */
#include <stdio.h>
#define EOL '\n'
main ()
{
char CHARACTER;
int A_COUNT, E_COUNT, I_COUNT,
O_COUNT, U_COUNT;
A_COUNT=0;
E_COUNT=0;
I_COUNT=0;
O_COUNT=0;
U_COUNT=0;
printf ("Enter line of text: \n");

do {
scanf ("%c", &CHARACTER);
    switch (CHARACTER)
          {
          case 'A':++A_COUNT;
          break;
          case 'E':++E_COUNT;
          break;
          case 'I':++I_COUNT;
          break;
          case 'O':++O_COUNT;
          break;
          case 'U':++U_COUNT;
          break;
          default: /* do nothing */;
}     } while (CHARACTER != EOL);
printf(" A = %d   E = %d   I = %d   O = %d   U = %d\n",
     A_COUNT, E_COUNT, I_COUNT, O_COUNT, U_COUNT);
}
```

(C) Going overboard

```
/*   program VOWELS   */

#include <stdio.h>

#define EOL '\n'

main ()
{
     char CHARACTER;
     int A_COUNT,
         E_COUNT,
         I_COUNT,
         O_COUNT,
         U_COUNT;

A_COUNT = 0;
E_COUNT = 0;
I_COUNT = 0;
O_COUNT = 0;
U_COUNT = 0;

printf ("Enter line of text: \n");
```

```
do
{
    scanf ("%c", &CHARACTER);
    switch (CHARACTER)
        {
        case 'A': ++A_COUNT;
                break;

        case 'E': ++E_COUNT;
                break;

        case 'I': ++I_COUNT;
                break;

        case 'O': ++O_COUNT;
                break;

        case 'U': ++U_COUNT;
                        break;

        default: /* do nothing */;
        }

} while (CHARACTER != EOL);
printf(" A = %d   E = %d   I = %d   O = %d   U = %d\n",
        A_COUNT, E_COUNT, I_COUNT, O_COUNT, U_COUNT); }
```

(D) Good prettyprinting

```c
/* program VOWELS */
#include <stdio.h>
#define EOL '\n'

main ()
{
    char CHARACTER;
    int A_COUNT, E_COUNT, I_COUNT, O_COUNT, U_COUNT;

    A_COUNT = 0;
    E_COUNT = 0;
    I_COUNT = 0;
    O_COUNT = 0;
    U_COUNT = 0;

    printf ("Enter line of text:\n");
    do {
        scanf ("%c", &CHARACTER);
        switch (CHARACTER) {
            case 'A': ++A_COUNT;
                    break;

            case 'E': ++E_COUNT;
                    break;

            case 'I': ++I_COUNT;
                    break;

            case 'O': ++O_COUNT;
                    break;

            case 'U': ++U_COUNT;
                    break;
            default: /* do nothing */;
        }
    } while (CHARACTER != EOL);
    printf(" A = %d   E = %d   I = %d   O = %d   U = %d\n",
            A_COUNT, E_COUNT, I_COUNT, O_COUNT, U_COUNT);
}
```

In our examples, we have attempted to incorporate certain prettyprinting examples. Appendix A itemizes some of these standards. We encourage the reader to make use of these standards. But keep in mind that standards (and automatic prettyprinting programs) only provide a minimum guide. It's the meaning that counts, both in the words and in the spaces. If the program you are writing has a good logical structure, then show it!

Proverb 14	***COMMENT FOR CONTENT***	*And none can read the text, not even I;* *And none can read the comment but myself.* ALFRED, LORD TENNYSON *Pelleas and Ettarer*

What the poet has to say above is, unfortunately, all too descriptive of too many programs written today. The myths surrounding the use of comments in programs is perhaps dispelled in this simple test:

True or false: A readable program is one with copious comments.

Answer: Usually, false

True or false: A good program may have no comments in the statement part.

Answer: Possibly, true.

Comments are a form of internal documentation that allows the programmer to describe the internal workings of a program. One example will suffice to make the point. Consider the program of Figure 3-5A. This program has no comments. The reader is invited to examine the program and determine the meaning of each statement.

Next, consider the program of Figure 3-5B. The comments convey the logical structure of the program. O.K. But they go too far. They are distracting and tell the obvious.

Figure 3-5C shows a deeper concern for the reader. The comments are clearly separated from the code and give more precise statements about the entire function, even telling us about Euclid's algorithms.

Figure 3-5.   *Use of effective comments*

(A) Poor solution: no comments

```
/* Program GCD_1 */
#include <stdio.h>

main ()
{
     int HI_VALUE, LO_VALUE, REMAINDER, GCD, N1, N2;

     printf ("Enter two positive integers: ");
     scanf ("%d %d", &N1, &N2);
     if (N1 <= N2) {
          LO_VALUE = N1;
          HI_VALUE = N2;
     } else {
          LO_VALUE = N2;
          HI_VALUE = N1;

     }

     do {
          REMAINDER = HI_VALUE % LO_VALUE;
          HI_VALUE = LO_VALUE;
          LO_VALUE = REMAINDER;
     } while (REMAINDER != 0);

     GCD = HI_VALUE;
     printf ("GCD is %d\n", GCD);
}
```

(B) Overdoing it (but good for teaching)

```
/* -- Program GCD_2
   -- Function to compute the greatest common divisor of
   -- two numbers using Euclid's algorithm. Euclid's algorithm
   -- is one of repeated division. */

#include <stdio.h>

main ()
{
     int HI_VALUE, LO_VALUE, REMAINDER, GCD, N1, N2;

     /* Get initial values. */
     printf ("Enter two positive integers: ")
     scanf ("%d %d", &N1, &N2);

     /* Place in order. */
     if (N1 <= N2) {
         LO_VALUE = N1;
         HI_VALUE = N2;
     } else {
         LO_VALUE = N2;
         HI_VALUE = N1;
     }

     /* Perform Euclid's algorithm until GCD is found. */
     do {
         REMAINDER = HI_VALUE % LO_VALUE;
         HI_VALUE  = LO_VALUE;
         LO_VALUE  = REMAINDER;
     } while (REMAINDER != 0);

     /* Print results. */
     GCD = HI_VALUE;
     printf ("GCD is %d\n", GCD);
}
```

(C) Best solution: careful commenting

```
/* -- Program GCD_3
   -- Euclid's algorithm for the greatest common divisor of:
   -- two numbers:
   -- (1) The higher number H is divided by the lower L.
   -- (2) If the remainder is zero, H is the GCD,
   -- (3) otherwise, repeat with L divided by the remainder. */

#include <stdio.h>

main ()
{
    int HI_VALUE, LO_VALUE, REMAINDER, GCD, N1, N2;
    printf ("Enter two positive integers: ");
    scanf ("%d %d", &N1, &N2);

    if (N1 <= N2) {
        LO_VALUE = N1;
        HI_VALUE = N2;
    } else {
        LO_VALUE = N2;
        HI_VALUE = N1;
    }

    do {
        REMAINDER = HI_VALUE % LO_VALUE;
        HI_VALUE  = LO_VALUE;
        LO_VALUE  = REMAINDER;
    } while (REMAINDER != 0);

    GCD = HI_VALUE;
    printf ("GCD is %d\n", GCD);
}
```

Although the value of using comments can be illustrated over and over again, the programmer is often tempted not to use them. After all, when a programmer is writing a piece of code, comments may not be needed. But how many times during coding does the programmer go back and try to figure out what has happened and what is left to do? And what about the next day? Or the next week? Or the occasion when you are asked to change someone else's program?

One additional proverb is useful here: *Temperance is moderation in all things*. Comments can be overused as well as misused. It is far better to use good prettyprinting and good mnemonic names rather than to clutter up your code with copious comments. Comments should convey useful information. Frequent comments like

```
/* Empty buffer */
CLEAR_BUFF (B);
```

not only clutter up your program but may completely discourage anyone from trying to wade through it.

Here are Henry's three rules for C comments:

1. Write header comments (for the main program or a function).

2. Do header comments before coding.

3. Try not to use any other comments.

Don't let rule 3 confuse you. Good code speaks for itself: if a piece of code needs a comment, it is likely that the code itself could be better.

In short, comments can promote the design of maintainable programs. They can make a difference. *Use them, temperately.*

Proverb 15   *MAKE CONSTANTS CONSTANT*

The result of this proverb is most valuable after a program is written, during program testing or maintenance. The essential idea is to make sure that all constant data items are recognized and given a name. Furthermore, no statement should modify these constant data items.

Consider the programming situation of Figure 3-6A. The programmer assumed that the table would always contain 50 items. The integer 50, besides its use in constructing tables, was used freely throughout the programs in computing averages and controlling conditions. When an increase in data items resulted in 100 items, changing the number 50 to 100 was a searching chore, for it was all too easy to miss an occurrence of the integer 50. This is not the case with Figure 3-6B, where a data name was created and given a value in the constant declaration.

Figure 3-6.   *Integer constants*

(A) Poor

```
main ()
{
    float TOTAL, AVERAGE;
    int I;
    float LIST[50];

    ...
    TOTAL = 0;
    for (I = 0; I < 50; ++I)
        TOTAL = TOTAL + LIST[I];
    AVERAGE = TOTAL / 50;
    ...
    printf ("\nAverage Value = %f\n", AVERAGE);
    ...
}
```

(B) Better

```
#define NUM_ITEMS 50

main ()
{
    float AVERAGE, TOTAL;
    int I;
    float LIST[NUM_ITEMS];

    ...
    TOTAL = 0;
    for (I = 0; I < NUM_ITEMS; ++I)
        TOTAL = TOTAL + LIST[I];
    AVERAGE = TOTAL / NUM_ITEMS;
    printf ("\n Average value = %f\n", AVERAGE);
    ...
}
```

Not all numbers should be named. Consider the simple code fragments of Figure 3-7. Here the gain is not clear. Reason? The conversion factor 9/5 and the base 32 stand for themselves.

Figure 3-7.   *Naming obvious constants*

(A) Poor

```
float CENTIGRADE (FAHRENHEIT)
    float FAHRENHEIT;
{
    return ((9.0/5.0)*(FAHRENHEIT - 32.0));
}
```

(B) Better?

```
#define CONV_FACTOR 1.8
#define BASE_VALUE 32.0

float CENTIGRADE (FAHRENHEIT)
    float FAHRENHEIT;
{
    return (CONV_FACTOR*(FAHRENHEIT - BASE_VALUE));
}
```

The real issue involved here concerns the so-called "magic numbers," numbers such as those used in Figure 3-8A, a problem derived from [Marcotty, 1977], where

```
typedef enum {TOO_SHORT, TOO_TALL, OVER_WEIGHT,
UNDER_WEIGHT, NORMAL} weight_status;
```

How many times while reading code have you been stumped by what 75 and 124.0 are all about? A preceding comment line might help, but isn't the alternative of Figure 3-8B much better?

The principle is this:

- If a number, character, or string has a meaning that is not self-apparent, might be changed, or is confusing on its own, name it.

Figure 3-8.   **Magic numbers**

(A) Poor

```
weight_status WEIGHT_CHECK(HEIGHT, WEIGHT)
     float HEIGHT, WEIGHT;

     /* -- Function to determine whether a man's weight lies
        -- within normal limits. For heights in the range of
           62 to 75 inches.
        -- On exit, WEIGHT_CHECK returns one of:
        --    TOO_SHORT, TOO_TALL, OVER_WEIGHT, UNDER_WEIGHT, NORMAL */
{
     if (HEIGHT < 62.0)
          return (TOO_SHORT);
     else if (HEIGHT > 75.0)
          return (TOO_TALL);
     else if (WEIGHT > (133.0 + 4.3*(HEIGHT - 62.0)))
          return (OVER_WEIGHT);
     else if (WEIGHT < (124.0 + 4.0*(HEIGHT - 62.0)))
          return (UNDER_WEIGHT);
     else
          return (NORMAL);
}
```

(B) Better

```
#define MIN_HEIGHT 62.0
#define MAX_HEIGHT 75.0
#define LO_WEIGHT  124.0
#define HI_WEIGHT  133.0
#define CONV_FAC_1 4.3
#define CONV_FAC_2 4.0
weight_status WEIGHT_CHECK (HEIGHT, WEIGHT)
     float HEIGHT, WEIGHT;

     /* -- Function to determine whether a man's weight lies within
        -- normal limits. For heights in the range of 62 to 75 inches.
        --
        -- On exit, WEIGHT_CHECK returns one of:
        --    TOO_SHORT, TOO_TALL, OVER_WEIGHT, UNDER_WEIGHT, NORMAL */

{
    if (HEIGHT < MIN_HEIGHT)
        return (TOO_SHORT);
    else if (HEIGHT > MAX_HEIGHT)
        return (TOO_TALL);
    else if (WEIGHT > (HI_WEIGHT + CONV_FAC_1*(HEIGHT - MIN_HEIGHT)))
        return (OVER_WEIGHT);
    else if (WEIGHT > (LO_WEIGHT + CONV_FAC_2*(HEIGHT - MIN_HEIGHT)))
        return (UNDER_WEIGHT);
    else
        return (NORMAL);
}
```

There are two good ways in C to name constants.

The first method is using initial values in declarations, for instance

```
float MIN_HEIGHT = 62.0;
```

Such a value will hold within the definition of a function.

The second method is using #define, for example,

```
#define NUM_ITEMS 50
```

The #define option is most useful for naming quantities that are used in numerous functions, for preprocessor lines apply to the remainder of a file. Typically, we may have

```
#define SOC_SEC_RATE 6.45
#define NUM_ITEMS 50
#define MAX_LINE_LENGTH 80
#define STD_INDENT 10
#define CONTROL_CHAR '@'
#define BLANK ' '
#define FILLER "     "
#define MARKER "**"
```

If the constants are used in several files, the constants can be defined in a separate file. When the constants are needed in another file, the file of constants can be "included," for example,

```
#include TABLE_DATA
```

where TABLE__DATA may contain #define's as well as other declarative items.

On the other hand, there will be a few (only a few) cases where a constant can stand on its own, for instance,

52   the number of cards in a deck.
9/5   Fahrenheit to centigrade conversion factor.
0   initial value of a sum.

Here, you have a choice, name it or not. (But don't name 0 as "zero.")

Perhaps Shakespeare's remark in one of his sonnets summarizes this proverb better: "A constant is a wondrous excellence." The moral is simple: a well-designed program isolates constant data items in a constant declaration. There are two advantages. First, program modification is easier. But more important, reading the program is not an exercise in detective work, i.e., it is not supposed to be a mystery for the reader. You will need more constant declarations, but this is a small, one-time price to pay for the long-term dividend of a logically organized program.

Proverb 16 *NAME ALL TYPES*

> *There are ways, but the Way is uncharted; There are names but not nature in words: Nameless indeed is the source of creation. But things have a mother and she has a name.*
> *LAO TZU*
> *The Way of Life, I*

What is an unnamed type? Look at the following:

```
typedef struct {
    int SUIT;
    int RANK
    } card_deck[52];

float A[NUM_TESTS];
card_deck D;
```

For the variable A, what is the *name* of its type? There is none. For D[2], what is its *name* of its type? There is none. Both have unnamed types.

Now consider the following:

```
typedef struct {
      int SUIT;
      int RANK;
} card_info;

typedef card_info card_deck[52];
typedef float     test_results[NUM_TESTS];

test_results A;
card_deck    D;
```

What is the name of type of A? "test__results." What is the name of type of D[2]? "card__info." Both now have named types.

Why should we name all types?

1. It is an easy thing to do.

2. Procedure and function parameters will be clearer with named types.

3. The name tells us what the type means.

Why is this proverb lost on most programmers? Maybe they haven't thought about it, maybe it takes a little extra effort.

It's a good idea. Try it.

Proverb 17 **GET THE SYNTAX CORRECT NOW**

Experience is the name everyone gives to their mistakes.
OSCAR WILDE
Lady Windemere's Fan, Act III

In C, there is a good deal of criticism about its syntax. There is also criticism, which is often passed off to a C compiler, for not helping with "obvious" program mistakes. But the wise programmer does not look for excuses.

Consider the program fragments of Figure 3-9A, which contain some simple syntactic errors. Figure 3-9B shows the corresponding corrected version. Errors like the ones in the first example should be screened out in advance by a careful programmer. It is our contention that no errors, no matter how trivial, should pass the attention of a good programmer, for it is possible that some of them may not be detected by the compiler and will appear only after a program is in full operation. More subtly, some of those "tiny" errors may be keys to larger problems.

Figure 3-9.   **Some simple syntactic errors**

(A) Wrong

```
1.   X ++= 1;

2.   INDEX int;

3.   for (I = 1, I <= N, ++I)

4.   if ( X =! Y)
         printf ("Unequal values\n");
```

```
5.   SORT(NAME[50])
         string NAME;

6.   SQUARE(A, Y)
         float A, Y;
     {
         Y = A*A;
     }

7.   X, Y, Z: float;
     Z = X / Y;

8.   if (A != 0.0) {
         X1 = B + (sqrt((B*B) - (4*A*(C))) / (2*A));
         X2 = B - (sqrt((B*B) - (4*A(C))) / (2*A));
     else
         X1 = -C / B;
         X2 = 0.0;
     }

9.   printf ("A poorly structured program is like a syntax, error\");

10.  #define PI = 3.14159;
     int I;
```

(B) Correct

```
1.   ++X;

2.   int INDEX;

3.   for (I = 1; I <= N; ++I)

4.   if (X != Y)
         printf ("Unequal values\n");

5.   SORT(NAME)
         string NAME[50];

6.   SQUARE(A, Y)
         float A, *Y;
     {
         *Y = A*A;
     }
```

```
7.   float X, Y, Z;
     if (Y != 0.0)
          Z = X / Y;
     else
          printf ("Attempt to divide by zero!\n");

8.   if (A != 0.0) {
          X1 = B + (sqrt((B*B) - (4*A*C) / (2*A));
          X2 = B - (sqrt((B*B) - (4*A*C) / (2*A));
     } else {
          X1 = -C / B;
          X2 = 0.0;
     }

9.   printf ("A poorly structured program is like a syntax error\n");

10.  #define PI  3.14159
     int I;
```

Sometimes we work away at a desk and the manual is out in the car. Rather than pause for a moment to ensure that a particular syntactic construction is correct, we press forward thinking that any trivial error will be caught during verification. Not so. The time to consider syntax is not while testing the completed program, but while preparing it. Keep the manual handy as you write the code. If you are not absolutely positive that the syntax of the statement you are writing is perfect, look it up. It only takes a few seconds, and your grasp of the language will improve with constant references to the manual. This work habit is all the more crucial if you are just learning C or if you have done considerable programming in another language with similar, but nevertheless, different syntactic constructs.

Why? Why not let the compiler find the errors? It is shocking how much time programmers squander at the terminal. There is always a reason. A short function here, ten lines there, a quick test run. It doesn't work. A quick fix. An integration error. A new run. On and on. . .

You can and should write programs that are completely free of syntactic errors on the first run. But to do so, you have to be convinced that you can indeed do it. Have someone else read the work you produce (Proverb 22). Just think of all the hours of terminal time you can waste tracking down simple syntactic errors, not to mention some severe run-time problems that can be caused by such "trivial" errors.

Proverb 18   *REMEMBER YOUR READER*

Whenever you teach, be brief, that your readers' minds may readily comprehend and faithfully retain your words.

HORACE
Epistles, I

Programmers have a desire to produce that one unique program which will establish for themselves a lasting reputation in the field. They do this by shortening the code, running the program faster, and using fewer variables. The result is more often a tarnished image because the benefits seldom outweigh the costs incurred. Resist this temptation; a good programmer writes code that is simple to read and focuses on the problem to be solved.

To avoid surprises for the reader, a programmer must be aware that part of his job is to map real-world entities (e.g., prices, temperatures, dollars, dates, and people's names) into the constructs of the C language (e.g., numbers and strings). A programmer must not only choose a particular representation for an entity but must make sure that an operation validly represented in C has meaning when applied to the original entity. For example, you can perform all arithmetic operations on numeric data. But while you can subtract two dollar amounts to get another dollar amount, it does not make sense to multiply two dollar amounts or to take the square root of a dollar amount.

More generally (see Figure 3-10), the input to any program represents some class of real-world entities: chess squares, wages, row numbers, cards, colors, and the like. A computation is required to transform these entities into other entities; for example, a chess move, an amount of money, a new row number, a card played, another color, and the like. The computer, however, can operate only in limited ways and on a limited set of entities like strings or integers. Thus, it is necessary to transform the real-world set of entities and operations into a program containing computer entities and operations. We shall say that a program is "straightforward" if each step in the computer algorithm

Figure 3-10. *Model for a typical programming task*

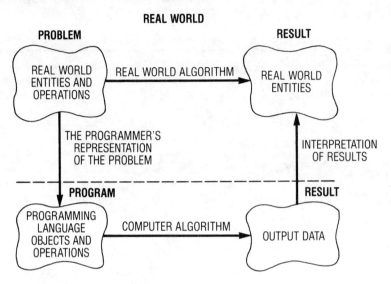

has a simple correspondence to a step in a real-world algorithm that a person would use to solve the problem.

Straightforwardness and naturalness are closely connected to the clarity and readability of programs. Any programmer soon learns that understanding another programmer's code is the "curse" of the profession. Often programs do not accurately reflect the real-world algorithm corresponding to the numerical, array, logical, or string operations that are required for their computer implementation.

Try looking at any program that you wrote a month ago without peeking at the comments or the documentation. See if you immediately understand all of its details. Now imagine what it would be like for someone else who hadn't seen the program before. Clarity is a godsend to anyone who has to document, debug, extend, use, grade, or otherwise handle a computer program. Unless a program printout is being used only by the original programmer, clarity is a double godsend to anyone having to use the program.

For example, consider the following problem. Given a deck of 51 cards, we are asked to find the rank of the missing card (by computer, of course!). The deck is stored in a 51-element array called DECK. To make things simple, a function GET__RANK__ NAME is assumed to be defined. GET__RANK__NAME takes the rank of a card (1 to 13) as its argument and maps the rank into a 6-character string:

```
"ACE  " for 1,
"TWO  " for 2,
...
"KING " for 13
```

Figure 3-11 depicts two pieces of code, both of which claim to do the job correctly. Your problem is to discover "why" each one gives the correct result.

Figure 3-11B is obviously correct. In the real world, it corresponds to keeping a checklist of each rank and checking off the card ranks, one by one, until the deck is exhausted. Then the checklist is scanned to find out which card has been checked fewer than four times, and the selected rank is printed.

Figure 3-11A is also correct but far less straightforward. It has little correspondence to typical card table operations. It runs through the deck keeping a modulo 13 count of all the ranks. Afterwards it subtracts this count from 13 to get the rank of the missing card. If you are not convinced, try it.

Figure 3-11. ***Two card-counting algorithms to find the rank of a missing card***

(A) Tricky card count

```
/* Program CARD_1 */
#include <stdio.h>

#define NUM_SUITS 4
#define NUM_RANKS 13
#define NUM_CARDS 51
#define DECK_SIZE 52

typedef struct {
     int SUIT_VAL;
     int RANK_VAL;
     } card_info;
typedef char rank_name[6];
typedef card_info deck_contents[DECK_SIZE];

...

main ()
{
     int I, RANK, COUNT;
rank_name NAME;
deck_contents DECK;

     ...
     COUNT = 0;
     for (I = 0; I < NUM_CARDS; ++I) {
          RANK  = DECK[I].RANK_VAL;
          COUNT = (COUNT + RANK) % NUM_RANKS;
     }
     NAME = GET_RANK_NAME(NUM_RANKS - COUNT);
     printf ("Missing rank is: %s\n", NAME);
}
```

(B) Natural card count

```
/* Program CARD_2 */
#include <stdio.h>
#define NUM_SUITS 4
#define NUM_RANKS 13
#define NUM_CARDS 51
#define DECK_SIZE 52

typedef struct {
     int SUIT_VAL;
     int RANK_VAL;
     } card_info;
typedef char rank_name[6];
typedef int rank_tally[NUM_RANKS + 1];
typedef card_info deck_contents[DECK_SIZE];

...

main ()
{
     rank_tally COUNT;
     int I, RANK;
     rank_name NAME;
     deck_contents DECK;

     ...
     for (RANK = 1; RANK <= NUM_RANKS; ++RANK)
          COUNT[RANK] = 0;
     for (I = 0; I < NUM_CARDS; ++I) {
          RANK = DECK[I].RANK_VAL;
          ++COUNT[RANK];
     }

     for (RANK = 1; RANK <= NUM_RANKS; ++RANK)
          if (COUNT[RANK] < NUM_SUITS)
          NAME = GET_RANK_NAME(RANK);
     printf ("Missing rank is: %s\n", NAME);
}
```

Another area where natural programs have an advantage is that of *extendability*. Because a natural algorithm is analogous to real-world operations, extensions using these operations can often be made easily. Since a tricky algorithm usually depends on specific properties of numbers or strings, it usually cannot be applied to cases other than the original problem.

The program of Figure 3-11 illustrates this point well. Say that we now wish to extend the given programs to find the ranks of missing cards from a deck containing fewer than 51 cards. The algorithm of Figure 3-11B can be extended quite readily, as shown in Figure 3-12. In the corresponding real world, the sweep of the checklist is the same as before except that when we find that a card is missing, we print it, and see if any others are missing.

Figure 3-11A *cannot* be extended, even to cover the case of two missing cards. The validity of the algorithm is based on the condition that there is only one missing card. With only one missing card, the difference between 13 and the count must be the rank of the missing card. With two or more missing cards, the sum of the ranks of the missing cards may be split in an arbitrary number of ways. In short, this algorithm fails because it is based on the particular properties of numbers instead of the properties of cards.

Before concluding the discussion of this proverb, remember that when you depart from a clear analogy with the problem, structure and clarity are frequently lost. Merging two or more modules of code in order to wring out those "extra lines" or adding a few lines in order to gain efficiency are both easy ways to prevent anyone from following the program. Considering the extra time needed to develop the special wrinkle and the extra testing time needed to check the new and often subtle boundary conditions, are you sure that fewer machine instructions or faster machine execution is likely?

There are cases where unusual methods are, in fact, justified, for example, to provide execution speed where it counts or economy of storage. However, before you resort to tricky programming, you should have a clear reason for doing so. Moreover, you should estimate the actual gain such programming will yield. Otherwise, you should stick to operations and objects that have a natural analogy in the real world.

Heed well, C programmers.

Figure 3-12.   *Extension of the natural card count*

```
/* Program CARD_3 */
#include <stdio.h>

#define NUM_SUITS 4
#define NUM_RANKS 13
#define DECK_SIZE 52

typedef struct {
    int SUIT_VAL;
    int RANK_VAL;
    } card_info;
typedef char      rank_name[6];
typedef int       rank_tally[NUM_RANKS + 1];
typedef card_info deck_contents[DECK_SIZE];

...

main ()
{
    rank_tally COUNT;
    int I, RANK, NUM_CARDS, NUM_MISSING;
    deck_contents DECK;
    rank_name NAME;

    ...
    for (RANK = 1; RANK <= NUM_RANKS; ++RANK)
        COUNT[RANK] = 0;

    scanf ("%d", &NUM_CARDS);
    for (I = 0; I < NUM_CARDS; ++I) {
        RANK = DECK[I].RANK_VAL;
        ++COUNT[RANK];
    }

    for (RANK = 1; RANK <= NUM_RANKS; ++RANK)
    if (COUNT[RANK] < NUM_SUITS) {
        NAME = GET_RANK_NAME(RANK);
        NUM_MISSING = NUM_SUITS - COUNT[RANK];
        printf (" %d missing with rank: %s\n", NUM_MISSING, NAME);
    }
}
```

Proverb 19   *YOUR OUTPUT IS NOT ONLY FOR YOU*

He has gained every point who has mixed practicality with pleasure, by delighting the reader at the same time as instructing him.
HORACE
Epistles, I

The best programmers that I have known have a bit of the poet in them: their output sings a little, rhymes a little. This quality often goes undetected by those who read the program later, who do not care how much time the programmer has spent in designing and debugging a program. The programmer who gets locked into a pattern of writing programs thinking only about results— the product that most people look for—generally produces output that pleases only the author and not the reader. Although the programmer knows what his program means and how to interpret the results, the same cannot be said for those who must wrestle with his product six months later.

    This is such an obvious proverb. With all the work and effort required to write a program, i.e., to solve a problem, why should the output of a complex challenge simply look like a slipshod effort because it is poorly spaced, messy, or skimpy? Look at Figure 3-13A. The output of this simple program is almost incomprehensible without an exact knowledge of the problem definition or the program itself. The output of Figure 3-13B, on the other hand, can be clearly understood by even the fledgling programmer.

Figure 3-13.   *Use of informative output*

(A) Poor

```
/* program REPORT_1 */
#include <stdio.h>
#define NUM_WEEKS 4
typedef int sales[NUM_WEEKS + 1];

sales WEEKLY_SALES;
int   SALESMAN, AVERAGE_SALE;
int   NUM_SALES, I;
```

```
int TOTAL_SALES (WEEKLY_SALES)
    sales WEEKLY_SALES;
{
    int I, TOTAL;

    TOTAL = 0;
    for (I = 1; I <= NUM_WEEKS; ++I)
        TOTAL = TOTAL + WEEKLY_SALES[I];
    return (TOTAL);
}

main ()
{
    scanf ("%d", &SALESMAN);
    for (I = 1; I <= NUM_WEEKS; ++I)
        scanf ("%d", &WEEKLY_SALES[I]);

    AVERAGE_SALE = TOTAL_SALES(WEEKLY_SALES) / NUM_WEEKS;

    printf ("%4d %d\n", SALESMAN, AVERAGE_SALE);
    for (I = 1; I <= NUM_WEEKS; ++I)
        printf ("%4d\n", WEEKLY_SALES[I]);
}

-- Output from Figure 3-13A

   4  1000
1030
 980
1000
 990
```

(B) Better

```
/* Program REPORT\2 */
#include <stdio.h>
#define NUM_WEEKS 4
typedef int sales[NUM_WEEKS + 1];

sales WEEKLY_SALES;
int   SALESMAN, AVERAGE_SALE;
int   NUM_SALES, I;

int TOTAL_SALES (WEEKLY_SALES)
    sales WEEKLY_SALES;
{
```

83

```
        int I, TOTAL;

        TOTAL = 0;
        for (I = 1;  I <= NUM_WEEKS; ++I)
            TOTAL = TOTAL + WEEKLY_SALES[I];
        return (TOTAL);
}

main ()
{
        printf ("Enter salesman id number: ");
        scanf ("%d", &SALESMAN);
        printf ("Enter each weekly sales amount: ");
        for (I = 1; I <= NUM_WEEKS; ++I)
            scanf ("%d", &WEEKLY_SALES[I]);

        printf ("\nSalesman %ld sold:\n", SALESMAN);
        for (I = 1; I <= NUM_WEEKS; ++I)
            printf ("    $%5d in week %ld\n", WEEKLY_SALES[I], I);

        AVERAGE_SALE = TOTAL_SALES(WEEKLY_SALES) / NUM_WEEKS;

        printf ("\n");
        printf ("Average weekly sales:  $%4d\n", AVERAGE_SALE);
}


-- Output from Figure 3-13B

Salesman 4 sold:
    $ 1030 in week 1
    $  980 in week 2
    $ 1000 in week 3
    $  990 in week 4


Average weekly sales:  $1000
```

The most pleasing poems and the most striking works of art have an organizing simplicity about them. They delight the reader and viewer as they instruct him. The moral of this proverb is that your output must be annotated so that it will stand on its own , not just for you but, if your effort is truly worthwhile, for all the future readers who will appreciate it.

Proverb 20 | *REVIEW, REVIEW, REVIEW* | *When I get an ancient edition, I have it copied; after it is copied, I have it checked; after checking, have it set up, after setup, have it checked again; after checking, have it printed; after printing, have it checked again. Even with such care, there are two or three percent typographical errors. In this matter, where the eyes face something directly and closely, there are mistakes.*

CHEN CHIJU, (1558 - 1639)
Yentse Yushih

The plight of this early Chinese writer is much the same as ours—and we have to solve our problems much the way he did, by reviewing again and again or, in our terms, by simply "hand-checking" the program. It is not easy to convince programmers that a program should be hand-checked before it is run. Yet run-time errors are the hardest to detect, and even if the system provides excellent debugging facilities, using the computer alone for this necessary review can be hazardous. The programmer may well be surprised at discovering errors like incorrect signs, infinite loops, and unusual conditions that lead to program crashes. More important, the benefit is that the programmer is likely to improve the program when it is seen in its "final" form.

The technique is simple. Choose a sample input, then calculate the output as if you were the computer, assuming nothing and using *exactly* what is written. See that each logical unit performs correctly and that the control sequence through the units is correct. If the program is too long or too complex to check in its entirety, then check each major section first, and later check the smaller units, assuming that the major units are correct. When choosing sample input, take special care to include the boundary conditions and other unusual cases. Failure to account for them is one of the most common programming errors.

For example, suppose you are writing a program that takes two nonnegative integers as input, a dividend and a divisor, and prints out two numbers—the integer part of the quotient and the integer remainder.

Assume that C does not have integer division and modulus operators. That is, given the integer variables DIVIDEND, DIVISOR, QUOTIENT, and REMAINDER, assume that you cannot just say:

```
QUOTIENT    = DIVIDEND / DIVISOR;
REMAINDER   = DIVIDEND % DIVISOR;
```

As a first pass, consider the program segment in Figure 3-14A. Does this work? No. Why not? Checking by hand, we find that the program runs into trouble at the while statement. REMAINDER is initially undefined. (Remember, never assume that the computer assumes anything.) So we change the program as shown in Figure 3-14B.

Does the program work now? Obviously not. Checking the boundary conditions by hand, we find that when the divisor is zero, the algorithm doesn't terminate. Since division by zero is undefined, we should process this case separately. It wouldn't be wise to leave the program in an infinite loop if we only considered the cost of computer time. So we change the program as shown in Figure 3-14C.

It still doesn't work. Checking another boundary condition, we find that if the divisor exactly divides the dividend, we always get a quotient of 1 less than the correct value. For example, 10 divided by 5 is always 2 with a remainder of 0 not 1 with a remainder of 5. Correcting this error is easy, as shown in Figure 3-14D.

Figure 3-14.   *Hand-checking a program*

(A) First attempt

```
/* program DIVIDE */
#include <stdio.h>

main ()
{
    int DIVIDEND, DIVISOR, QUOTIENT, REMAINDER;

    printf ("Enter dividend and divisor: ");
    scanf ("%d %d", &DIVIDEND, &DIVISOR);

    QUOTIENT = 0;
```

```
    while (REMAINDER > DIVISOR) {
        REMAINDER -= DIVISOR;
        ++QUOTIENT;
    }
    printf ("Quotient = %d, Remainder = %d\n", QUOTIENT, REMAINDER);
}
```

(B) Second attempt

```
/* program DIVIDE */
#include <stdio.h>

main ()
{
    int DIVIDEND, DIVISOR, QUOTIENT, REMAINDER;

    printf ("Enter dividend and divisor: ");
    scanf ("%d %d", &DIVIDEND, &DIVISOR);

    QUOTIENT = 0;
    REMAINDER = DIVIDEND;
    while (REMAINDER > DIVISOR) {
        REMAINDER -= DIVISOR;
        ++QUOTIENT;
    }
    printf ("Quotient = %d, Remainder = %d\n", QUOTIENT, REMAINDER);
}
```

(C) Third attempt

```
/* program DIVIDE */
#include <stdio.h>

main ()
{
    int DIVIDEND, DIVISOR, QUOTIENT, REMAINDER;

    printf ("Enter dividend and divisor: ");
    scanf ("%d %d", &DIVIDEND, &DIVISOR);

    if (DIVISOR == 0)
        printf ("Attempt to divide by 0.\n");
    else {
        QUOTIENT = 0;
        REMAINDER = DIVIDEND;
```

```
        while (REMAINDER > DIVISOR) {
                ++QUOTIENT;
                REMAINDER -= DIVISOR;
        }
        printf ("Quotient = %d, Remainder = %d\n", QUOTIENT, REMAINDER);
    }
}
```

(D) Fourth attempt

```
/* program DIVIDE */
#include <stdio.h>

main ()
{
    int DIVIDEND, DIVISOR, QUOTIENT, REMAINDER;

    printf ("Enter dividend and divisor: ");
    scanf ("%d %d", &DIVIDEND, &DIVISOR);

    if (DIVISOR == 0)
        printf ("Attempt to divide by 0.\n");
    else {
        QUOTIENT  = 0;
        REMAINDER = DIVIDEND;
        while (REMAINDER >= DIVISOR) {
                ++QUOTIENT;
                REMAINDER -= DIVISOR;
        }
        printf ("Quotient = %d, Remainder %d\n", QUOTIENT, REMAINDER);
    }
}
```

Proverb 21	***CAREFUL PROGRAMMERS DON'T HAVE ACCIDENTS***	*What in hell have I done to deserve all these kittens.* DON MARQUIS *Mehetibel and her kittens*

The top-down approach to programming is the answer to the question: "What have I done?"—a question that may not need to be asked at all if the approach is followed conscientiously. The top-down approach is not only an effective tool in program development, but it is just as valuable in program verification. This simply means that the main program and upper levels are verified first and the most primitive modules last.

Top-down testing is a strategy which says

- Test a given module *before* testing any modules that it calls.

Figure 3-15.   *Picture of a program designed top-down*

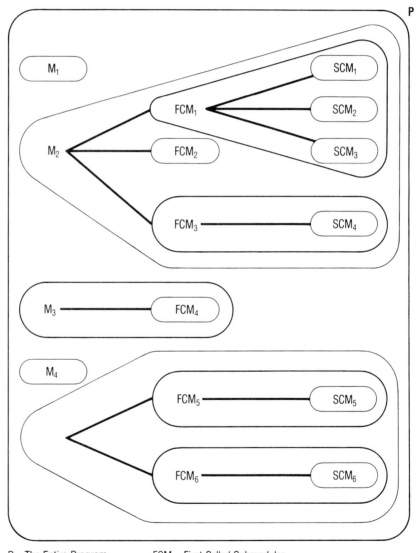

P—The Entire Program   FCM—First Called Submodules
M—Main Modules   SCM—Second Called Submodules

Verifying from the top down should seem obvious, especially if a program is being written top-down. Programs of this type are usually well modularized, and it is unwise to verify lower levels if the upper levels may be incorrect. Since the sections of the program are integral units that can stand on their own, the most important ones should be verified first. A schematic illustration of a program is presented in Figure 3-15. Encircled sections indicate that the set of enclosed modules is to be considered as a unit. The program has five main modules, each of which can be verified separately. The verification process starts with the main program. As an upper module is verified, the process continues through lower levels until the entire program has been verified. Verifying the entire program in one lump is to be avoided.

Consider Figure 3-16, a program for summing the first N positive integers for differing values of N. Clearly, the answers generated by the program are incorrect. The programmer decides to check the main program loop and adds the verification lines shown, which print out the inner loop control variable and the current value of the sum. When the revised program is run, we can easily see that on iteration 1 for the second value of N, the sum is already 22; that is, SUM is not properly initialized. Moving the SUM initialization statement to just before the inner for loop solves the problem.

One popular verification aid available in several implementations is the "trace." Basically, a trace is a facility which will monitor the behavior of prespecified variables or functions. The trace of a variable can monitor any use or change of its value. The trace of a function can monitor each call, its arguments, and its returned value. The programmer can use a trace to verify that functions are being called with proper arguments and correct returned values. In function-oriented programs or programs using recursion, traces can be invaluable.

Systems that implement C ordinarily offer other verification facilities. Does your system support any program design, development, or documentation aids? Does your system support a cross-reference lister, program librarian, test data generator, test supervisor, module testing, execution monitor, or output analyzer package? Be sure to find out what features your system

Figure 3-16.   *Use of the print statement for verification*

```
/* Program SUM */
/* Program to sum the first N positive integers. */
#include <stdio.h>
main ()
{
     int SUM, I, J, N;
     int NUM_SEQUENCES;

     printf ("Enter number of sequences: ");
     scanf ("%d", &NUM_SEQUENCES);

     SUM = 0;
     for (I = 0; I < NUM_SEQUENCES; ++I) {
          printf ("Enter number of terms: ");
          scanf ("%d", &N);
          for (J = 1; J <= N; ++J) {
               SUM += J;
          }
          printf ("Sum of first %d integers is %d\n", N, SUM);
     }
}

-- Output from Figure 3-16

Sum of first 6 integers is 21
Sum of first 3 integers is 27

-- Verification line inserted within inner loop:
   printf ("Iteration %d, Sum %d\n", J, SUM);

-- Output from Figure 28 with Verification Line

Iteration 1 Sum 1
Iteration 2 Sum 3
Iteration 3 Sum 6
Iteration 4 Sum 10
Iteration 5 Sum 15
Iteration 6 Sum 21
Sum of first 6 integers is 21
Iteration 1 Sum 22
Iteration 2 Sum 24
Iteration 3 Sum 27
Sum of first 3 integers is 27
```

provides, and incorporate them into programs you write. Some implementations of C have excellent run-time aids. Although it may not be wise to use implementation-dependent features as part of a final program, it would be foolish not to utilize them for verification.

There is no doubt that you will ask yourself "What have I done?" many times in program verification. But if you make the best use of the verification facilities in your computer system, you will know what you have done. One who expects the worst is doubly blessed; even when the worst happens, you will be prepared. If the best is your lot, you will be quietly proud that neither result was an accident.

4 *AND OF COURSE...*

Let us hear the conclusion of the whole matter.
Ecclesiastes 12:13

Proverb 22 | ***HAVE SOMEONE ELSE READ THE WORK*** | *An old man has crossed more bridges than a young man has crossed streets.*
CHINESE PROVERB

The sequence of these proverbs is a matter of choice, but if there is one "proverb among proverbs" for programmers, it should be this one. Few programmers can, or should, enjoy any kind of "poetic license" in their work—the parameters of the discipline demand that one's effort be open for inspection and criticism. In fact, this proverb should be understood as a requirement of good practice as much as any proverb that has gone before.

Having someone else read the work does *not* mean just having someone else read the final code. Even a developing definition should be read by someone else, as well as the program specifications, the levels of the top-down design, and the test plans.

The benefits of a second reading are legion: identifying unwarranted assumptions, unintentional omissions, unnecessary complexities, or just plain mistakes. But more important, both you and your reader will improve your problem-solving and programming techniques by this kind of mutual involvement. This is the principle of programming teams that is so important in fostering cooperative communication, maintaining team standards, promoting quality documentation, and generally keeping abreast of the total work effort.

Consider Figure 4-1, which contains two simple errors—both easy to make and both difficult to detect. The programmer who wrote the code would find the errors almost impossible to detect by rereading the code even one more time. Try to find them yourself.

Figure 4-1. *The compiler catches one error, but who catches the other?*

```
/* -- Program ROOTS
   -- Finds the real roots of the equation:
   --    A*(X*X) + (B*X) + C = 0 */
#include <stdio.h>
#include <math.h>

main ()
{
    float A, B, C, Z;
    float X1, X2;
    float DISCRIMINANT;

    printf ("Enter A, B, and C: ");
    scanf ("%f %f %f", &A, &B, &C);

    if (A == 0.0)
       if (B == 0.0)
            printf ("This is the degenerate case");
       else {
            X = -C / B;
            printf ("One real root. . . X = %d", X);
         }
    if ((A != 0.0) && (B != 0.0)) {
        DISCRIMINANT = (B*B) - (4*A*C);

        if (DISCRIMINANT < 0.0)
            printf ("No real roots.\n");
        else if (DISCRIMINANT == 0.0) {
            X1 = -B / 2*A;
            X2 = X1;
            printf ("Equal real roots: X1 = %f X2 = %f", X1, X2);
        } else if (DISCRIMINANT > 0.0) {
            X1 = (-B + sqrt(DISCRIMINANT)) / 2*A;
            X2 = (-B - sqrt(DISCRIMINANT)) / 2*A;
            printf ("Distinct real roots: X1 = %f X2 = %f", X1, X2);
        }
    }
    printf ("\n");
}
```

Here are a few suggestions to make your work-reading more effective:

a. Make sure you have a piece of work in *writing*.

b. Don't give someone else 20 pages at a time; 3 or 4 will do.

c. Focus on the work itself, not on the persons or personalities that produced it.

d. Do it on a regular basis: put it in your plan.

e. Don't confuse work-reading with a "meeting"—it is not a structural function, it is a good programming habit.

f. Take special care in looking for missing details, fuzzy statements, and boundary conditions.

If the piece of work is too long or too complex to check in its entirety, check each major section first—or better, just remember the last proverb.

Work-reading requires extra time and demands extra care, but it is a small price to pay for the benefits listed above. At first, the practice may seem time consuming, annoying, and even embarrassing at times. But given time, abiding with this proverb will have a marked impact on your work. You should practice as a reader for others, too. You will find, as I have, that *all aspects of good programming practice are improved by work-reading.* In no time at all, you will be crossing more bridges than streets—and you don't have to be an old man to do it.

Proverb 23

WHAT HAVE YOU READ LATELY?

No book is worth anything until it is worth much; not is it serviceable until it has been read, and reread, and loved, and loved again; and marked, so that you can refer to the passages you want in it.
JOHN RUSKIN
Sesame and Lilies,
Of Kings' Treasuries, Sect. 32

A friend of a friend was taking a year off and was asked, in an offhanded manner, what was he looking forward to the most? He said, "Oh, of course, to read! Teaching does not give one the chance to read. I'm always afraid I may have missed something."

This is what this proverb is all about—reading. There are two facets to reading:

a. *Technical*: the reading associated with your system— language reference manuals, system manuals, utilities manuals, operating and environment guides.

b. *Literary*: the reading associated with your field— magazines, journals, and books.

The objectives are:

a. To become a master of the system.

b. To develop better perspectives.

The common failures are:

a. Clinging to a timid subset of a system.

b. Becoming a "hacker" of the trade.

Nothing can be as boring as system manuals. Why go back to read them again? Because somewhere in all those poorly written manuals, the same kind that you are dedicated to improve, there is a kernel of knowledge that you may have overlooked. After programming for a while, we tend to settle into our own kind of convenient language for our host computer. Periodically rereading the manuals helps to remind us that there are many useful features that, even though we don't use them every day, may be just the ones we need later.

For example, do you know how C deals with control characters? Do you know how integer division works? Do you know all the predefined functions and the file manipulation capabilities? How does your implementation allow setting up of program libraries? How about the number of significant figures kept by your particular machine? How do enumeration types really work on your implementation? Can input or output files be structured or segmented? What are the default specifications for output of standard data types? Do you know what the maximum integer is?

As you survey the literature, you will encounter the writings of programmers of many stripes: hackers, boring, introverted, machinelike, uncultured, and so on. These impressions need not be true as you read more deeply into their writings. Programmers who publish do so to advance their profession because they understand that their experience is as beneficial to their peers as the writings of their mentors was to them. While there is no substitute for project experience, our own skills will be improved by reading. Consider:

a. an article on professional ethics;

b. an experiment on the philosophies of command languages;

c. a report on a new printer;

d. a book on software engineering;

e. data on which features of System X are little used;

f. a report on typical C enhancements;

g. a curriculum for computer science;

h. a product review.

These can be worth reading, even when they may be only marginal to your current project.

The question is: What is the state of the art? As you make your contribution, you must read to see what other contributions are being made. Rereading your own manuals and the current literature goes with the territory. You may be pleased at what you find.

| Proverb 24 | *DON'T BE AFRAID TO START OVER* | *To dry one's eyes and laugh at a fall, and baffled, get up and begin again.*
ROBERT BROWNING
Life in a Love, Stanza 2 |

Odd as it may seem, the first and last of these proverbs are encouraging! Don't panic and don't be afraid to start over! I say this because I hope that you should never have to lean on either proverb—all the ones that come between should be enough support.

Sometimes during program development, testing, or modification, it may seem that the program you are working on is becoming unusually cumbersome. So many user-requirements changes may have been thrown at you that the problem itself is different from the original proposal. Other than the first and last, maybe none of these proverbs seemed to apply in developing the program and the result is that the program produces error after error.

No matter. At some point, pruning and restoring a blighted tree is an impossible task—better to replace it with a seedling. The same is true of blighted computer programs. Restoring a structure that has been so distorted by patches and deletions or trying to find a program with a seriously weak algorithm simply isn't worth the time. The best that can result is a long, inefficient, unintelligible program that defies even more maintenance.

You have to develop a heartless sense of recognizing that when the program is hopelessly in trouble, chuck it out and start over again. And don't let your ego stand in the way. The lessons that you learned on the old program can be applied to the new one and yield the desired result in far less time with far less trouble.

Use these two proverbs to advantage. Don't panic, and start over. Above all, don't try to convert a bad program into a good one—bring out a new model.

EXERCISES FOR PART 1

Exercise 1 *Problem Definitions*

Consider the following program specification:
"Write a program that computes the weight in kilograms of a weight expressed in pounds and ounces."
Upon careful thought, the above specification reveals many points that would be unclear to a programmer. Rewrite the above specification so that *any* two programs written to solve the problem would have *exactly* the same input-output characteristics, for example, the same input format, the same number of significant digits, the same headings, and so forth. (Note: You are to write a program specification, *not* a program; a good definition may require a full page.)

Exercise 2　*Problem Definitions*

Each of the following program specifications is either missing one or more critical definitions or is unclear, misleading, or confusing. (a) How are the program specifications deficient? (b) Rewrite all or part of one program specification to make it as clear and explicit as possible, that is, so that there can be no doubt as to what the program should do. (c) In general, what does *any* program specification require to make it as clear and explicit as possible?

Program specification 1: Given the following rates of payment, write a program that will compute the monthly commission for a car salesman.

Grade of Salesman	Commission Rate
1	$5.00 + 0.50% for first ten sales $7.50 + 0.75% every subsequent sale
2	$7.50 + 0.75% for first ten sales $10.00 + 1.00% every subsequent sale
3	$10.00 + 1.00% for first ten sales $12.50 + 1.25% every subsequent sale
4	$12.50 + 1.25% for first ten sales $15.00 + 1.50% every subsequent sale
5	$15.00 + 1.50% for first ten sales $17.50 + 1.75% every subsequent sale

The input should be the grade of the salesman and the number of sales he has made for the month. The output should read "THE SALESMAN'S COMMISSION IS $ C," where C is the salesman's commission.

Program specification 2: The Programmer's Equity Life Insurance Company offers policies of $25,000, $50,000, and $100,000. The cost of a policyholder's annual premium is determined as follows. There is a basic fee that depends upon the amount of coverage carried. This is $25 for a $25,000 policy, $50 for a $50,000 policy, and $100 for a $100,000 policy.
In addition to the basic fee, there are two additional charges de-

pending on the age and lifestyle of the policyholder. The first additional charge is determined by multiplying the basic fee by either 1½, 2, or 3 if the policy is at the $25,000, $50,000, or $10 0,000 level, respectively. The second additional charge is determined by the policyholder's lifestyle, which is a rating of the danger of harm resulting from his occupation and hobbies. This rating is determined by company experts from a questionnaire returned by the policy applicant. They return a rating from 1 to 5 in steps of 1, with 1 being the safest rating. The charge is then determined by multiplying this rating by 5 and then further multiplying by 1½, 2, or 3 if the policy is either at the $25, 000, $50,000, or $100,000 level, respectively. The total premium is found by adding together these separately determined charges.

Write a program to output tables of yearly premium costs for persons of ages from 21 to 75 for all amounts of policy value and safety ratings.

Exercise 3   *Perfect Problem Specifications*

Upon extremely careful reading, the problem definition of Figure 1-2 shows several deficiencies. The *exact* input-output characteristics are not really fully specified. Describe these deficiencies.

Exercise 4   *Functions and Procedures*

Consider a program with the following specifications:

Input: a positive integer N
Output: the values SUM(N), SUM^2(N), SUM^3(N), and SUM^4(N)

where SUM(N) denotes the sum of the first N integers, SUM^2(N) denotes SUM(SUM(N)), and so forth.

1. Write the program *without* the use of functions.

2. Write the program using functions.

The differences can be quite striking.

Exercise 5   *Goto's*

Restructure the following statements to eliminate all goto's and statement labels and to make the sequence as *short* and clear as possible. (Note: Can it be done with only two assignment statements?)

```
        goto L3;
    L1: if (X == 0)
            goto L9;
        else
            goto L5;

    L5: if (X > MAX_VALUE)
            goto L6;
        else
            goto L4;

    L9: printf ("%g", X);
        goto L7;

    L3: scanf ("%g", &X);
        goto L1;

    L6: X = sqrt(X);

    L8: X = X*X + X;
        goto L9;

    L4: X = X*X;
        goto L8;

    L7: /*do nothing*/;
```

Exercise 6   *Goto's*

Consider the conventional 8 by 8 array representation of a chessboard whose squares are denoted by (1,1), (1,2), . . ., (8,8) and the problem of placing eight queens on the board so that *no* queen can capture *any other* queen. In chess, a queen can capture an other piece if the queen lies on the same row, column, or diagonal as the other piece.

1. Write a program to read in the coordinates of eight queens and print "TRUE" if no queen can capture any other, and "FALSE" otherwise.

2. Draw a flow diagram for the program.

3. Score the program using the formula
   SCORE = 100 - 10*(number-of-crossing-lines)
   as applied to the diagram.

Exercise 7   *Syntax*

It is important that a programmer be able to detect simple syntactic errors. Consider the following program to compute PI using the series,

$$PI^4/96 = 1/1^4 + 1/3^4 + 1/5^4 + \ldots.$$

How many syntactic errors are there? Correct the program fragment so that there are no errors.

```
N = 0;
while (ABS(TEMP) < EPSILON) {
      ++N;
      TEMP = 1 / (2N - 1)**4;
      SUM  += TEMP;
}
PI = sqrt(sqrt(96*SUM));
```

Exercise 8   *Syntax*

Which of the following examples are syntactically correct instances of the given C categories? Correct the erroneous examples. If possible, you should assume *any* suitable specification statements needed to make a construct correct. That is, the question is "Is there any conceivable program where the construct could be correct?"

1. *Arithmetic Expression*

   ```
   F(F)
   ```

2. *Arithmetic Expression*

```
P[Q] + X**X**X - 1/2
```

3. *If Statement*

```
if (X && Y > 4)
    printf ("%f", X);
```

4. *For Statement*

```
for (I == 1; I = N; ++I)
    X[I] = X[I] + X[I];
```

5. *Type Declaration*

```
typedef enum {TRUE, FALSE} boolean;
```

6. *Switch Statement*

```
switch (COLOR) {
    case RED:    GREEN;
    case GREEN:  printf ("GO");
    case YELLOW: printf ("SLOW DOWN");
    case RED:    printf ("STOP");
    break;
}
```

7. *Function*

```
float F(X, Y, Z);
    float X, Y, Z;
{
    return (X*Y + Z);

}
```

8. *Function*

```
float F(X, Y, Z)
    float X, Y, Z;
{
    float SUM;
```

```
                    for (I = 0; I < Z; ++I)
                            SUM += X[I] + Y[I];
                    return (SUM);
            }
```

9. *Assignment Statement*

```
    I = F[I].B[I]
```

10. *Compound Statement*

```
    {
            typedef enum {RED, WHITE, BLUE color;
            color C;
            ...
            if (C < RED)
            ...
    }
```

Exercise 9   *Mnemonic Names*

The following statement sequence performs a well-known, simple arithmetic computation. By basically changing all identifiers, rewrite the program so that it clearly illuminates the intended computation.

```
    /* program STRANGE */
    #include <stdio.h>
    #include <math.h>

    #define FOUR 4
    #define FIVE 3
    #define AND "and"

    main ()
    {
            float LEFT, RIGHT, MIDDLE, ONE, ALL, LEFT_1,
                LEFT_2, RIGHT_1;

            printf ("Enter three values: ");
            scanf ("%g %g %g", &LEFT, &MIDDLE, &RIGHT);
            RIGHT_1 = LEFT*RIGHT*FOUR;
            LEFT_1  = MIDDLE*MIDDLE - RIGHT_1;
            LEFT_2  = sqrt(LEFT_1);
```

```
ONE     = -(MIDDLE - LEFT_2)/(FIVE*LEFT);
ALL     = -(MIDDLE + LEFT_2)/(2.0e0*LEFT);
printf ("%g %s %g", ONE, AND, ALL);
}
```

Exercise 10 *Change*

Consider a program to compute the gravitational force F exerted between two planets M1 and M2 located (over time) at different orbital distances from each other. In particular, let

M1 = mass of planet 1 $= 6 * 10^{24}$
M2 = mass of planet 2 $= 8 * 10^{25}$
G   = gravitational constant $= 6.7 * 10^{-11}$
F $= G * M1 * M2 / (R^2)$

Write a program to output F for values of R varying from $100*10^8$ to $110*10^8$ in increments of $0.01*10^8$ such that all constants are named and *no* constant terms are recomputed.

Exercise 11 *Output*

The following input/output was generated by the use of a working interactive program:

```
Input:   What is N1 and N2?
         5, 10

Output:  5             25
         6             36
         7             49
         8             64
         9             81
         10            100
```

Rewrite the input/output so that the average "man on the street" would be able to understand what the input numbers 5 and 10 represent and what the output means.

Exercise 12   *Work Reading*

Describe two more advantages to having someone else read the work you produce during the various phases of a programming project. Describe two disadvantages or bottlenecks.

Exercise 13   *Reading the Manuals*

Reread your C manual and find three features that you had forgotten or did not know existed. For each feature, give an example of how it would be useful.

Exercise 14   *Reading the Manuals*

Answer precisely the following questions with reference to your C implementation:

1. What type names are predefined?

2. How many dimensions can an array have?

3. What is a legal subscript?

4. Are matrix commands available?

5. How many significant digits are kept for real numbers?

Exercise 15   *Code Rewrite*

The following program performs a simple, well-known computation. Rewrite the program so that it clearly illuminates the intended computation. In the process, eliminate goto's, use mnemonic names, and produce good output.

```
/* Program GOTOS */
#include <stdio.h>

main ()
{
```

```
        float A, B, C, D, F, G;

        goto L1;

    L2: scanf ("%f", &A);
        F = A * A;
        goto L3;

    L1: scanf ("%f", &B);
        G = B * B;
        goto L2;

    L3: if ((A <= 0) || (B <= 0))
            goto L5;
        else {
            C = F + G;
            D = sqrt(C);
            printf ("The answer is %g", D);
        }

    L5: /*exit*/;
    }
```

Exercise 16 *It Worked the First Time*

Write a program that determines whether an input string is a palindrome. A palindrome is a string that reads the same forward and backward. For example, LEVEL is a palindrome but PALINDROME is not. When the program is running correctly, score it using the following formula:

SCORE = 100 − (5*times-resubmitted)
            − (2*number-of-lines-changed)

Exercise 17 *Intermediate Variables*

Usually a complex mathematical expression can be coded as a single arithmetic expression. However, for the sake of clarity it is often advantageous to split up a lengthy arithmetic expression and use intermediate variables. Give an example where clarity is gained with the use of intermediate variables. Give an example where the obvious result is program efficiency. Give an example where the use of inappropriate or excessive intermediate variables causes confusion.

Exercise 18 *Guess the Proverb*

The following program is supposed to have the following characteristics:

Input: a sequence of n nonzero integers terminated by the integer zero

Output: the MEAN (the sum of all values divided by n)

$$SUM(x) / n$$

and standard deviation,

$$sqrt(SUM(x^2) / n - MEAN^2)$$

of the integers in the input sequence.

```c
/* program STATISTICS */
#include <stdio.h>
#include <math.h>

main()
{
    int A, B, C;
    float D, E, F, G;

    A = 0; B = 0; C = 0;
    D = 0; E = 0; F = 0;

    do
    {
        scanf (%f, &G);
        while (G != 0) {
            A = A + G;
            C = C + G*G;
            scanf ("%f", &G);
            ++B;
        }
    } while (G >= F);
```

```
    D = A/B;
    E = sqrt(C/B - sqr)(A));
    I = F - D/F;
    printf ("Mean is %g Deviation is %g", D, E);
}
```

Of all the programming proverbs, which *single* proverb, if properly followed, would be most valuable in converting the above program to a good program? (Note: There really *is* a best answer.)

Exercise 19 *The C Quiz*

A user who has a very thorough knowledge of any language should be able to detect erroneous programs that prematurely terminate because of a syntactic (compile-time) or semantic (run-time) error. In the absence of a formal definition of a language, the definition of constructs that produce fatal syntactic or semantic errors must ultimately be based on a particular implementation. To treat this issue precisely, consider the insertion of print statements as the first and last executable statements in a program, and let us adopt the following definitions:

1. A program is "syntactically invalid" if the first print statement is not executed, that is, if the implementation finds an unacceptable error.

2. A program is "syntactically valid" if the first print statement is executed, that is, if the implementation detects no severe errors, translates the program into machine language, and begins execution.

3. A program is "semantically invalid" (but syntactically valid) if the first but not the last print statement is executed, that is, the program is started but not completed.

4. A program is "semantically valid" (and syntactically valid) if the first and last print statements are executed, that is, if the program is executed without abnormal termination.

To test your knowledge of the above issues in C, you are asked to answer two simple questions about the programs given in the C quiz below.

Is the first printf statement (which prints "Start") executed?
Is the last printf statement (which prints "Finish") executed?

Check the appropriate spaces or put your answers on a separate sheet. Note: It is quite difficult to answer all questions correctly.

1. Start: YES____   NO____
   Finish: YES____   NO____

```
/* program ONE */
#include <stdio.h>

main ()
{
    int A, B, C;

    printf ("Start \n");
    A = 1;
L6: B = 2;
    goto L6;
L6: C = 3;
    printf ("Finish \n");
}
```

2. Start: YES____   NO____
   Finish: YES____   NO____

```
/* program TWO */
#include <stdio.h>
float X;

float MAX_VALUE (X, Y)
    float X, Y;
{
    if (X < Y)
        return (X);
    else
        return (Y);
}

float P(F)
    float (*F)();
{
```

```
        return ((*F)(1.4, 2.6));
}

main ()
{
        printf ("Start\n");
        X = P(MAX_VALUE);
        printf ("Finish\n");
}
```

3. Start: YES____   NO____
   Finish: YES____   NO____

```
/* program THREE */
#include <stdio.h>

P(X, Y)
    float X, *Y;
{
    ++X;
    *Y *= (X + 1);
}

main ()
{
        float A;
        printf ("Start\n");
        A = 2;
        P(A, 1);
        printf ("Finish\n");
}
```

4. Start: YES____   NO____
   Finish: YES____   NO____

```
/* program FOUR */
#include <stdio.h>

#define FALSE 0
#define TRUE 1

P(X, Y)
     float X, *Y;
{
```

```
            ++X;
            *Y *= (X + 1);
      }

      main ()
      {
            float A;

            printf ("Start\n");
            A = 2;
            P(A, &TRUE);
            printf ("Finish\n");
      }
```

5. Start: YES____   NO____
   Finish: YES____   NO____

```
      /* program FIVE */
      #include <stdio.h>

      int G(N)
            int N;
      {
            if (N == 0)
                  return (1);
            else
                  return (N*G(N-1));
      }

      int FACT(N)
            int N;
      {
            return (G(N));
      }

      main ()
      {
            int J;

            printf ("Start\n");
            J = FACT(5);
            printf ("Finish\n");
      }
```

6. Start: YES____ NO____
   Finish: YES____ NO____

```
/* program SIX */
#include <stdio.h>

main ()
{
      typedef float boolean;
      boolean B;

      printf ("Start\n");
      B = 14.2;
      printf ("Finish\n");
}
```

PART
TWO

BEYOND THE PROVERBS

5 *PROGRAM STANDARDS*

*We come from a world where we have known
incredible standards of excellence.*

> Thornton Wilder
> *The Bridge of San Luis Rey, Chapter 4*

The C language has been with us for many years, yet the writing of high-quality C programs has remained a matter of personal style. The thrust of this chapter is to go beyond the "proverbs" and present some rigorous standards for the writing of C programs. Developing rigorous program standards is not easy, for the rules must be unambiguous. They must also be of sufficient merit that a programmer will not be unduly stifled by their adoption. We have followed this chapter's standards throughout this book.

The importance of developing such standards is clear. For managers, instructors, and programmers, there is a need to develop uniform rules so that everyone may more easily understand programs, a need to develop coding techniques that reduce the complexity of programs, and a need to control the entire software development effort.

I make no attempt here to encompass the numerous features of the C language. No standard can cover every aspect of a given programming problem. Nevertheless, the standards presented here should go part way to promote quality programs.

The general issue of programming standards is indeed complex. When the initial boundaries of a language are restricted, the programmer resistance can be great. In addition, any attempt to promote or enforce such a set of standards must resolve a number of difficult issues.

First, exceptional cases must be avoided when writing a standard. It is critical that the standard be as solid as possible, for otherwise, the credibility of the entire activity can be undermined. Possible exceptional cases must thus be carefully screened before the standard is adopted.

Second, there is the issue of enforcement. What mechanism should be set up to enforce the standards? Can the standards really be enforced without some kind of automatic aids? What about the professional programmer who does not see any reason for a particular standard or its use in a particular case? These questions are difficult to answer.

Third, given that some method of enforcement has been adopted and given that some useful exception does occur, how is the exception to be handled? While an ideal standard has no exceptions, when exceptions do arise, they have to be handled without undermining the credibility of the entire effort.

Fourth, there are a number of human factors that must be faced, especially when standards are being developed. For one, choices may be a matter of taste, and there are bound to be some arbitrary decisions. Further, there may be some initial overhead in following the standards. The human tendency is to get on with the job, i.e., code. This tendency must be resisted, for if the standards are correct, breaking the standards is shortsighted.

Finally, one must be very careful to avoid expecting too much from the standards, for eventually the problem-dependent features of a program will demand special attention. While the adoption of good standards may help in producing good solutions to the problem at hand, ultimately the style and expertise of the practicing programmer becomes paramount.

GENERAL REQUIREMENTS

[Gen-1]   *Someone Should Be Appointed To Maintain and Enforce the Standards.*

The rationale here is to refine the standards, monitor them, and allow exceptions, but *only* in a controlled manner. It is critical that all programming standards, unless revoked, be followed to the very last detail. The method for enforcing the standards is left to the particular instructor, team leader, or manager.

[Gen-2] *All Full Programs Shall Include Header Comments.*

For example:

```
/* -- ** PROGRAM TITLE:     Brief title
   --
   -- ** WRITTEN BY:        Name of author(s)
   -- ** DATE WRITTEN:      Date
   --
   -- ** PROGRAM SUMMARY:   Brief program summary
         . . .
   -- ** INPUT AND OUTPUT FILES:
   --       file-name:      Brief description of use
         . . .
 */
```

The rationale here is to give at least a minimum synopsis of the program's intent, input and output files, and title information, so that a program has some minimal internal documentation.

[Gen-3] *For Each Application There Should Be an Adopted Set of Standard User-Defined Names and Abbreviations.*

The standard words should be chosen *before* coding. The following set of names is a very small sample of those that might be adopted for an application.

SYM	Abbreviation for *symbol*
MSG	Abbreviation for *message*
NUM	Abbreviation for *number*
POS	Abbreviation for *position*
GET_SYM	For a subroutine to input symbols
SYM_LENGTH	For lengths of symbols
PUSH	For a subroutine to put symbols on a stack
POP	For a subroutine to remove symbols from a stack
STACK	For a stack of attributes
KEY_VALUE	For an array of keyword values

119

```
DIGIT           For numeric characters
LETTER          For alphabetic characters
E OF_MSG        For an end-of-file message
```

The rationale here is to develop a well-accepted set of naming conventions and to reduce the time spent by programmers in devising good mnemonic words. This standard is intended to promote program readability and to prevent confusion caused by having different names for the same entities.

[Gen-4] *Multiline Comments Must Begin Each Full Line with a Double Hyphen (--).*

[Gen-5] *All Comments Should Be Written in Upper/ Lowercase.*

[Gen-6] *Reserved Words and Preprocessor Keywords Are To Be Written in Lowercase.*

[Gen-7] *The Words of a Compound Name Are To Be Separated by Underscores.*

The idea here is to make the comments visually separate from the program itself, and make programmer names clear and visible. Thus instead of something like

```
/* Find next root. */       -- Case 1
interval = epsilon;
estimate = f(x2 - x1) / 2.0;

if (nextchar == line[i])    -- Case 2
      length++;
else
      length--;
use
```

```
/* Find next root. */       -- Case 1a
Interval = Epsilon;
Estimate = F(X2 - X1) / 2.0;
```

```
/* -- Find next root. */      -- Case 1b
INTERVAL = EPSILON;
ESTIMATE = F(X2 - X1) / 2.0;


if (next_Char == Line[I])      -- Case 2a
    Length++;
else
    Length--;


if (NEXT_CHAR == LINE[I])      -- Case 2b
    LENGTH++;
else
    LENGTH--;
```

The latter are easier on the reader.

[Gen-8] ### *No Program Unit Should Exceed Two Pages in Length.*

The rationale here is to force program units (i.e., main programs, functions, or definitions) to be isolated on at most two pages of text. In general, each program unit should occupy no more than a single page of text. However, due to cases where initializations or repeated computations require extensive code, the standard allows program units to occupy up to two pages of text.

[Gen-9] ### *Each Function Should Begin on a New Page, or (for Short Functions) with a Break of at Least Three Blank Lines.*

If you have ever spent ten minutes trying to locate a function in a long listing, you will believe the wisdom of this rule.

[Gen-10] ### *Each Line Should Have Fewer than 80 Characters.*

This one sounds easy, but many programmers use wide printers that can take 120 characters per line. So, why not go beyond 80 characters? Because

1. Long lines get hard to read.

2. Huge indents happen too easily.

3. Most copiers use standard (8.5 inches by 11 inches) paper.

4. Large pieces of paper are cumbersome for filing.

And most importantly,

5. There just is no need.

It's silly to break this rule.

[Gen-11]   *Each Statement Must Begin on a Separate Line.*

This means that

```
COUNT = 1; SUM = 0;
```

and

```
while (NEXT_CHAR != BLANK) {scanf("%c", &NEXT_CHAR);
    COUNT++;}
```

are not allowed. The point is that such statements can be over-looked. Placing each on a new line, i.e.,

```
COUNT = 1;
SUM   = 0;
```

and

```
while (NEXT_CHAR != BLANK) {
    scanf ("%c", &NEXT_CHAR);
    COUNT++;
}
```

makes a simple rule that the reader can depend on. Programmers in a hurry like to break this rule.

[Gen-12] *Expressions May Not Produce Any Internal Side Effects.*

This means no input, output, or updates of variables are allowed within the middle of an expression. This rules out

```
while (*BUFFER++ = *CH++);
    /* Copy characters */
```

and

```
CH = NEXT(GET_CHAR());
```

but not

```
CH = GET_CHAR();
```

This is a very tough rule to live by, but is well worth it.

DECLARATIONS

[Dcl-1] *Except for Self-Identifying Values, All Scalars (Numbers and Characters) That Remain Constant Throughout a Program Must Be Named.*

The rationale here is to isolate constants and, if need be, to allow changes without affecting the logic in the executable statements. For example, use

```
int   MAX_ITEM_NUM  =  100;
float EPSILON       = 0.001;
char  CONTROL_CHAR  = '@';
...
NUM_HITS = 0;
for (I = 0; I < MAX_ITEM_NUM; ++I) {
    if (A[I] < EPSILON)
            ++NUM_HITS;
    ...
}
```

rather than

```
NUM_HITS = 0;
for (I = 1; I < 100; I++) {
    if (A[I] < 0.001)
            ++NUM_HITS;
  ...
}
```

The #define facility is another fine way to name constants, especially for constants used in more than one subprogram. The exception allows values like 52 (for the number of cards in a deck) to remain unnamed.

[Dcl-2]   *Except for "Static" Variables, Program Variables May Not Be Initialized in Their Declarations.*

This means that

```
int TOTAL = 0;
...
TOTAL += I;
```

is not allowed. Some programmers will dislike this rule. The rationale is to initialize variables near the sections of code where they are updated. The rationale is also to force a clear distinction between variables and named constants.

[Dcl-3]   *All Types Must Be Named.*

The rationale here is to be clear about the use of types. Instead of

```
int OCCUPIED[32];
struct move_pair {
    int SQ1;
    int SQ2;
} LEFT_JUMP[32];
```

use

```
typedef int status_flags[32];
```

```
typedef struct
    {int SQ1;
     int SQ2;} move_pair;
typedef move_pair adjacent_sqs[32];

status_flags OCCUPIED;
adjacent_sqs LEFT_JUMP;
```

This rule forces a uniformity and simplicity that ultimately saves a good deal of time and promotes readability.

[Dcl-4]

A (User-Defined) Function May Not Change the Values of Its Arguments.

The rationale here is to force a pure use of functions called within expressions, that is, to eliminate side effects within functions. For example, the function

```
int OCCURS (SEARCH_CHAR, CHAR_STR, STR_LENGTH, ERROR)
    char SEARCH_CHAR;
    char CHAR_STR[];
    int STR_LENGTH;
    status ERROR;

{
    . . .
    if (COUNT > STR_LENGTH) {
        ERROR  = TOO_LONG;
        return (0);
    } else
        return (COUNT);
}
```

is not allowed. Instead, a procedure or "void" function (with no return value) must be used.

[Dcl-5]

The Parameters of a Procedure Should Be Declared with Comments Describing the Logical Role of Each Parameter.

The rationale here is to give some minimal information on the logical role of the subprogram. For example, use

```
EXAMPLE (/*in*/      A, B,
         /*in-out*/  C, D,
         /*out*/     E, F)
```

The comments /*in*/, /*in-out*/, and /*out*/ may be replaced by more informative comments, for example: /*using*/, /*updating*/, and /*giving*/. Pure (value-returning) functions need not follow this rule.

[Dcl-6]   *Each Field in a Record Should Be Declared on a Separate Line.*

This is a small point. It means use

```
struct COORD {
    int X;
    int Y;
}
```

not

```
struct COORD {
    int X, Y;
}
```

The symmetry of separate fields better illuminates the logic of the structure.

[Dcl-7]   *Declarations May Not Be Used within a Nested Compound Statement.*

This means using

```
int I;
...
if (X > XMAX) {
    for (I = 0; I < N; I++)
        VALUE(I) = 0.0;
        ...
}
```

not

```
if (X > XMAX) {
     int I;
     for (I = 0; I < N; I++)
          VALUE(I) = 0.0;
          . . .
     }
```

The rationale is that this use of the scope rules just goes too far.
Scope has its purpose, but also its limits. The simple model of a
module consisting of (a) declarations, followed by (b) statements
is a good one.

[Dcl-8]

Functions Used To Return Values Must Have an Explicitly Declared Result Type. Functions Used as Procedures May Not Return a Value.

Thus use the headers

```
int STACK_SIZE (S)
     stack S;
GET_SYMBOL (B, SYM)
     buffer B; symbol_info SYM;
```

not

```
STACK_SIZE (S)                    /* Do not assume int */
int GET_SYMBOL (B, SYM);          /* Do not return a
                                     value here */
```

STATEMENTS

[Stm-1]

Goto and Continue Statements Are Not Allowed. Except within Switch Statements, Break Statements Are Not Allowed.

The rationale here is to force the programmers to *think ahead*
and use only 1-in, 1-out control structures. Many programmers
at first believe that this restriction is unreasonable. With some

practice, programming with these control structures becomes quite easy. If it seems necessary to use one of these statements, the following alternatives should be considered:

1. Restructuring the algorithm.

2. Putting blocks of code in a subroutine.

3. Copying in a piece of code.

4. Repeating a condition previously tested.

5. Reversing a condition to its negative.

If you think you need a Goto or Break for efficiency, any savings will be tiny. If pushed to the wall, perhaps you should be using assembly language.

Note: Break statements are allowed (in fact, necessary) to complete a Switch statement.

[Stm-2]   ***Nesting of Any Combination of If, For, While, Do, and Switch Statements Must Be No More Than Four Levels Deep. A Generalized Decision Structure Simulating a "Select-First" Is Counted as One Level.***

The rationale here is to prevent the human complexity that results from deeply nested control structures. If statements that simulate a generalized decision structure are conceptually one level. For example,

```
if (case-1)
    statement-1;
else if (case-2)
    statement-2;
...
else if (case-n)
    statement-n;
```

counts as one level of nesting. It is surprising how easily this generally accepted rule is broken.

[Stm-3] *Null Statements Must Include a Comment Line.*

For example, use

```
switch (J) {
    case 1: DOTHIS;
            break;
    case 2: X = X + 1;
            break;
    case 3: printf ("%d", X);
            break;
    case 4: /* no action */;
}
```

The rationale here is to make a null action explicit.

[Stm-4] *Compound Looping Statements Are Displayed with Indented Bodies. The Opening Brace Is on the Header Line; The Closing Brace Is after the Last Statement.*

This means using

```
while (X < Y) {
    statement-1;
    statement-2;
    statement-3;
}
for (I = 0; I < NUM_ITEMS; I++) {
    statement-1;
    statement-2;
    statement-3;
}

do {
    statement-1;
    statement-2;
    statement-3;
} while (C != TERMINATOR);
```

The rationale is to give loops a parallel form, to minimize indentation and extraneous blank lines, and give visually clear bracketing.

[Stm-5] *If Statements Are Displayed in a Comblike Fashion Rather Than a Nested Fashion.*

I can't figure out how to say this in any clear way, but it means using this:

```
if (WEATHER == SUNNY) {    /* -- single choice */
    FINISH_CHORES;
    OVEN = OFF;
    TAKE_ABREAK;
}

if (WEATHER == SUNNY) {    /* -- binary choice */
    FINISH_CHORES;
    OVEN = OFF;
    TAKE_A_BREAK;  }
else {
    CLEAR_KITCHEN;
    OVEN = ON;
    START_COOKING;
}

if (WEATHER == SUNNY) {    /* -- another possibility */
    FINISH_CHORES;
    OVEN = OFF;
    TAKE_A_BREAK;
} else {
    CLEAR_KITCHEN;
    OVEN = ON;
    START_COOKING;
}
```

There is no real optimum layout for C. The rationale is to prevent tricky indentation.

[Stm-6]   *The Bodies of Compound Statements, Loop Statements, as Well as the Bodies of Structures, Must Be Indented from Their Corresponding Headers and Closing Brackets.*

This prohibits

```
{
X = 1;
Y = 1;
}
```

and

```
    while (CH != SPACE) scanf ("%c", &CH);
```

and

```
    struct { int X;
             int Y; }
```

Rather, use

```
{
    X = 1;
    Y = 1;
}
```

and

```
    while (CH != SPACE)
        scanf ("%c", &CH);
```

and

```
    struct {
        int X;
        int Y;
    }
```

The rationale is to force a consistent layout.

131

[Stm-7]   *The ++ and −− Operations Are Only Allowed in Prefix Form for Solo Assignment Statements.*

Of the following cases

```
++COUNT;
--COUNT;
TALLY = ++COUNT;
TALLY = COUNT++;
TALLY = COUNT--;
TALLY = --COUNT + I;
```

the first two are allowed. The assignments to TALLY must be spelled out in other ways. The rationale is to reduce some of the unwarranted trickery in programs.

SPACING

[Space-1]   *A Uniform Indentation of Three to Five Spaces Is to Be Used.*

Programmers vary their indentation conventions all over the lot, which is senseless. Three, four, or five spaces are perfect, and lovely for the reader. Examples are:

```
MAIN ()                 /* -- Case 1. Variables */
    int SUM;
    char NEXT_CHAR;

typedef struct {        /* -- Case 2. Structure fields */
    unsigned ADDRESS:8;
    unsigned REGISTER:2;
    unsigned OP_CODE:6;
} word;

if (X > Y)              /* -- Case 3. Then-part */
    printf ("X and Y are %f and %f", X, Y);

SPACE_ALERT ()          /* -- Case 4. function body */
{
```

```
        printf ("Almost totally out of space. \n");
        return;
}

while (X > Z) {          /* -- Case 5. Loops */
        ++COUNT;
        X = X + F(X);
}
```

[Space-2] *At Least One Space Is Put Before and After Each Relational Operator (for Example, ==, <, and <=) and After Each Binary + and − Operator.*

Obvious? No. You will often see

```
    DATA[I] = COUNT+VALUE;
```

or

```
    if (X==Y) . . .
```

But the problem gets worse in

```
    NUM2 = 10*DIGIT_VAL(CHAR_3)+DIGIT_VAL(CHAR_4);
```

and

```
    if (NEXT_APPROX(X,Y,EPSILON)>1.0) . . .
```

The rule is ever so simple, almost a courtesy to the reader. It is not worth breaking.

[Space-5] *A Space Should Be Used as in Normal English Usage.*

It's elementary, but violated all the time. The rule applies to cases like

```
    /*An inline comment*/
```

133

```
for (X=10; . . .
```

which are better written as

```
/* An inline comment */

for (X = +10; . . .
```

6 *POTPOURRI*

A little learning is a dangerous thing;
Drink deep, or taste not the Pierian spring.

Alexander Pope
Essay on Criticism, Part I

The five topics discussed in this chapter:

> global variables,
> selecting mnemonic names,
> recursion,
> efficiency, and
> the case against program flowcharts.

should not mislead the reader as being secondary to the proverbs of Part One. Nor should the title "potpourri" be taken as though these vital topics are afterthoughts in the issues of C programming today. On the contrary, a separate chapter is needed beca use these topics require and deserve a deeper discussion than the more succinct vehicle of the proverbs allows.

GLOBAL VARIABLES

The use of variables to represent updated entities is familiar to all programmers. Guidelines for the effective use of variables are seldom discussed. Nevertheless, this topic is of paramount importance.

In what follows, I am going to make some rather strong statements against the use of global variables. This is a controversial area. Before we get going, I would like to make a point that gets to the heart of this book. It is about the nature of how people read and comprehend programs.

Consider any "block" of code (i.e., a sequence of statements), B. The block B performs some computation, F, on two variables, x1 and x2, to yield a result, y, as illustrated in Figure 6-1. In any such block there may, of course, be other intermediate variables needed for the computation. Assume for the moment that each of the intermediate variables is not used outside the block of code B except for one variable, V. In order to abstract the computation F in B, one must then not only consider the computation of y from x1 and x2, but *also* consider the effect on V. Our simple mental model is lost. In this case we say that v is "active in" or "global to" the block.

Figure 6-1.   ***Mental abstraction***

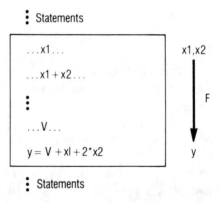

The use of global variables is a frequent cause of complexity in computer programs. To abstract the computation of a logical block of code, the uses of global variables must be considered.

There are several problems associated with global variables. First, the complexity of a block of statements rapidly increases with even a small increase in the number of variables. Second, if the number of statements over which the variables range is large, then the intent of referencing statements can be difficult to comprehend. Third, any change to a program outside the block of statements can affect the correctness of the block itself.

The concept of global variables in C is most evident in the case of variables that are declared outside a function or procedure.

The examples which follow take advantage of this circumstance. But the concept should be understood in terms of *any* block of code that has the *effect* of a unit of computation.

As mentioned earlier, C does not make the following (commonly held) distinction. A "function" refers to a subprogram that returns a value. A "procedure" refers to a subprogram that produces a change in a variable outside the subprogram. In particular, consider the simple declaration of Figure 6-2. In Figure 6-2A, the subprogram AREA is used as a function. For example, if the value of R is 3.0, an evaluation of the expression

```
1.0 + AREA(R)
```

yields one, plus the value of the function. In Figure 6-2B, the subprogram AREA is used as a procedure. For example, if the value of R is 3.0, the statement

```
GETAREA (R, &AREA)
```

results in assigning to AREA the value computed by the procedure. The difference between functions and procedures is important but not always obvious. Generally speaking,

- functions are used in place of *expressions* to return *values*, whereas,

- procedures (void functions) are used in place of *statements* to perform *assignments* to variables.

Figure 6-2.   *Functions versus procedures*

(A) A simple function

```
#define PI 3.14159

float AREA (RADIUS)
    float RADIUS;
{
    return (PI * (RADIUS*RADIUS));
}
```

(B) A simple procedure

```
#define PI 3.14159

void GET_AREA (RADIUS, AREA)
     float RADIUS, *AREA;
{
     *AREA = PI * (RADIUS*RADIUS);
}
```

It is possible in C to write subprograms that both return a value and cause an effect outside the subprogram. As a rule, it is unwise to do this, as we shall see in subsequent examples.

Note: Strictly speaking, the main program in C is a function, called "main." In this work I have normally declared the variables for the main program outside (i.e., before) the function "main." I do not consider this a use of global variables, but the thoughtful reader may prefer to restructure the main programs.

Context Effects

Loosely speaking, the *context* of a subprogram is its relation to other sections of a program. If a subprogram alters a quantity global to itself, then it exhibits a *context effect*. Basically a subprogram can produce a context effect in three ways:

1. by altering its arguments,

2. by altering a global variable,

3. by *using* a global variable that is changed   between calls.

Case (2) is known as a "side effect." In case (3), not at all harmless, the damage comes from outside the subprogram.

Programmers who write subprograms with context effects can get unpleasant surprises. Consider Figure 6-3. These two programs are identical except for the replacement of the expression

```
F(B) + F(B)
```

in Figure 6-3A by the expression

```
2*F(B)
```

in Figure 6-3B. These two programs are not equivalent because

Figure 6-3.   *Context effect on the returned value of a function*

(A) One program

```
/* program ADDITION_1 */
#include <stdio.h>

int A, B, C;
int F(X)
    int X;
{
    ++A;
    return (A * X);
}

main ()
{
    A = 10;
    B = 3;
    C = F(B) + F(B);      /* use of F */
    printf ("%d\n", C);
}
```

(B) An equivalent program?

```
/* program ADDITION_2 */
#include <stdio.h>

int A, B, C;

int F(X)
    int X;
{
    ++A;
    return (A * X);
}

main ()
{
    A = 10;
    B = 3;
    C = 2 * F(B);    /* use of F */
    printf ("%d\n", C);
}
```

```
F(B) + F(B) == (11)*(3) + (12)*(3)
                 == 69
2*F(B)           == (2)*(11)*(3)
                 == 66
```

Hence, we lose a fundamental property of addition. The problem is caused by the context effect in the function F with the assignment of (A + 1) to A, where A is global to the function.

A similar case arises in Figure 6-4. These examples are also identical except that

```
F(B) + G(B)
```

in Figure 6-4A is replaced by

```
G(B) + F(B)
```

in Figure 6-4B. Using a left-to-right evaluation, the written values for C, 72 and 75, are not the same. Here, the familiar commutative property of addition is lost because of the assignment to a global variable. Certainly many programmers would be surprised to learn that F(B) + G(B) is not equivalent to G(B) + F(B). Since C employs conventional mathematical notation, it is dangerous to write functions that violate the properties of established mathematical systems.

Figure 6-4.   ***Context effect by assignment to a global variable***

(A) One program

```
/* program ADDITION_3 */
#include <stdio.h>

int A, B, C;

int F(X)
     int X;
{
     ++A;
     return (A * X);
}
```

```
int G(X)
     int X;
{
    A += 2;
    return (A * X);
}

main ()
{
    A = 10;
    B = 3;
    C = F(B) + G(B);    /* calls to F and G */
    printf ("%d\n", C);
}
```

(B) An equivalent program

```
/* program ADDITION_4 */
#include <stdio.h>

int A, B, C;
int F(X)
     int X;
{
    ++A;
    return (A * X);
}

int G(X)
     int X;
{
    A += 2;
    return (A * X);
}

main ()
{
    A = 10;
    B = 3;
    C = G(B) + F(B);    /* calls to F and G */
    printf ("%d\n", C);
}
```

Next consider Figure 6-5, a case in which a function subprogram alters the value of an argument. The problem here is that two function calls with the same arguments return *different* values. In larger programs, such a use of arguments is quite dangerous. In making a correction or alteration, the programmer may unwittingly alter the value of calls to the function. Furthermore, to replace F with another procedure, the programmer must consider the main program in order to ensure the proper handling of global variables.

Figure 6-5.   *Context effect on the arguments of a function*

```
/* program SIDE_EFFECT */
#include <stdio.h>

int A, B, C;

int F(X, Y)
    int X, *Y;
{
    *Y += X;
    return (X * *Y);
}

main ()
{
    A = 4;
    B = F(2, &A);    /* gives 12 */
    C = F(2, &A);    /* gives 16 */
    printf ("%d %d\n", B, C);
}
```

Lastly, consider Figure 6-6, where a similar thing happens, only here the effect comes from *outside* the function. It's the same problem.

The purpose of a procedure is to produce some effect external to itself, not to return a value. Essentially, a procedure consists of a group of statements isolated from a main routine or program for convenience or clarity. The problems encountered with context effects in procedures are quite similar to those encountered in functions. There is one important exception. Since a procedure is designed to update a specific set of variables, each of the changed variables should be included in the list of arguments. Consider Figure 6-7. By using all assigned variables in the argument list in each procedure call, the reader can speed up tracing the changed variables, since he or she will not have to look through the body of the procedure.

Figure 6-6.   ***Context effect from outside a subprogram***

```
/* program TROUBLE */
#include <stdio.h>

int A, B, C;

int F(X)
    int X;
{
    return (X * A);
}

main ()
{
    A = 1;
    B = 2;
    C = F(B);
    printf ("%d\n", C);    /* gives 2 */

    A = 2;
    C = F(B);
    printf ("%d\n", C);    /* gives 4 */ }
```

The case against context effects becomes even more severe when we need to change a program. Change is a daily occurrence in programming. Someone may find a more efficient algorithm, more output may be needed, a bug may be detected, or revised specifications may be given. If a piece of code to be changed has context effects, then those effects must be accounted for. The resulting changes may imply the need to delve deeply into the entire program for a clear understanding of what effects a function or procedure has on other parts of the pro-

---

Figure 6-7.   *Context effect in procedures*

(A) Poor

```
/* program HIDDEN_PARAMETER */
#include <stdio.h>

int A, B;

P (X)
     int *X;
{
     *X = 2 * (*X + 1);
     B = 5 * *X;
}

main ()
{
     A = 4;
     B = 3;
     P(&A);
     printf ("%d %d\n", A, B);    /* B is not 3 */
}
```

(B) Better

```
/* program EXPLICIT_PARAMETER */
#include <stdio.h>

int A, B;

P (X, Y)
     int *X, *Y;
{
     *X = 2 * (*X + 1);
     *Y = 5 * *X;
}

main ()
{
     A = 4;
     B = 3;
     P(&A, &B);                  /* tells about B */
     printf ("%d %d\n", A, B);
}
```

---

gram. Adding a few extra lines of code for that desirable change may kill the correctness of another piece of code. As a result, another change may be needed to right matters, and so on. Even if this process succeeds, it is not likely to add to the clarity or flexibility of the program. Had the original program been written without context effects, the subprogram could be changed *without* looking at the rest of the program.

There are, of course, cases where global entities may indeed be useful. For example, there may be arrays whose (often used) values remain constant within the program. Making these quantities global to the entire program certainly causes no problems. The global use of the legal move mappings in the Kriegspiel program illustrates this point. These are *not* really global variables, but global *constants*.

Global variables and context effects can cause serious problems. If they are used, they should be used sparingly. In summary, I give the following rules of thumb:

1. Functions
Do not use a function when you need a procedure.
Use a function only for its returned value.
Do not alter formal parameters.
Do not use any global variables.

2. Procedures (void functions)
Do not use a procedure when you need a function.
Do not use global variables.
Put all outside variables in the parameter list.

3. Both
Be very careful if you ever use global variables.

SELECTING NAMES

When writing C programs, it is tempting to use short and often uninformative user-defined names. An extra effort is required to devise and actually code more illuminating (usually, but not always, longer) names. Nevertheless, the choice of names has a long-lasting impact that cannot be ignored. Consider the two toy programs in Figure 6-8. Of the two, Figure 6-8B is the more lucid procedure for reading a sequence of numeric values and printing the maximum.

Figure 6-8.   *Using mnemonic names*

(A) Poor

```c
/* program BIG_1 */
#include <stdio.h>

int N, INDEX;
float  X, BIG;
main ()
{
     printf ("Enter length of sequence: ");
     scanf ("%d", &N);
     printf ("Enter first number: ");
     scanf ("%d", &X);
     BIG = X;
     for (INDEX = 1; INDEX < N; ++INDEX) {
          printf ("Next number: ");
          scanf ("%f", &X);
          if (BIG < X)
               BIG = X;
     }
     printf ("The largest value = %f\n", BIG);
}
```

(B) Better

```c
/* program MAX */
#include <stdio.h>

int NUM_VALUES, I;
float NEW_VAL, MAX_VAL;

main ()
{
     printf ("Enter length of sequence: ");
     scanf ("%d", &NUM_VALUES);
     printf ("Enter first number:);
     scanf ("%f", &NEW_VAL);
```

```
    MAX_VAL = NEW_VAL;
    for (I = 1; I < NUM_VALUES; ++I) {
        printf ("Next number: ");
        scanf ("%f", &NEW_VAL);
        if (MAX_VAL < NEW_VAL)
            MAX_VAL = NEW_VAL;
    }
    printf ("The largest value = %f\n", MAX_VAL);
}
```

Good mnemonic names are a powerful tool for clear documentation, easy verification, and ready maintenance. I offer several basic naming principles:

1. Choose names that activate the correct "meaning" or "psychological set" [see Weinberg, 1971].

2. Try to use short, full names.

3. Use standard names and abbreviations.

4. Follow consistent naming conventions.

5. Avoid names that can be confused with a system name, that are unpronounceable, or that are otherwise unfortunate.

Meaning

In psychology, the term "psychological set" means a readiness to respond in a specific way to certain stimuli. In the programming context, a "psychological set" means a readiness to associate particular entities or properties with a word. Entities such as social security numbers, rates of pay, and people's names have many possible word representations. It is important that the psychological set activated by a particular name be "correct" (i.e., suggest the intended entity). Of course, the psychological set activated by a particular name differs for different people.

We start with a simple example. Suppose you use the identifier

```
N_CHAR
```

in a program. What would you think? Some possibilities are:

    a. the number of characters?

    b. a number for a character?

    c. an n-character array?

Right off, you say the name is poor. Now what about

```
GET_COORD
```

Looks better. It is probably a procedure to get a coordinate.

But there is a big point here. Programmers should always choose names that activate the precise meaning. Some rules are:

    a. Decide *exactly* what is to be named.

    b. Choose a name that says it.

    c. Look at the name as it appears in the code and ask if the *reader* will be able to conclude the same thing.

Rule (c) is the key.

When you read something like

```
if (A[N_CHAR] == B[COUNT])
```

chances are you have problems. But when you see something like

```
GET_COORD(XPOSITION, YPOSITION)
```

or

```
if (COUNT[NEXT_CHAR] == MAX_ALLOWED)
```

the going is probably a lot easier. This is what naming is all about.

Creating a name with the correct psychological set can be difficult. Often it is easy to pick a name with a close but dangerously incorrect psychological set. As an example, suppose a programmer decided to represent a file of sale transaction items, and the record's three fields (the identification of the salesperson, the identification of the item sold, and the quantity of the item sold) with the respective names TRANS__FILE, FIELD__1, FIELD__2, and FIELD__3. The name TRANS__FILE might cause a reader to associate the following

    a. a transit file,

    b. transactions of any sort,

    c. transportation records,

and so on. A better choice would be SALE__FILE, and even better, SALES__FILE or SALES__DATA. Likewise, the data names FIELD __1, FIELD__2, and FIELD__3 are less clear than PERSON__ID, ITEM__ID, and NUM__SOLD.

Short, Full Names

Another aspect of naming arises when names have no specific semantic role. For example, a programmer may define an array whose subscripts do not correspond to any meaningful object in the real world, or may define a function of purely mathematical arguments. In both cases, a standard name should be used. For example, subscripts are generally denoted by I, J, or K; functions by F, G, or H; and arguments by X, Y, or Z. Often these familiar conventions will lend understanding. For example,

```
I = F(X, Y)
```

is more suggestive than

```
Y = X(I, F)
```

if the left-hand side denotes an integer-valued variable and the right-hand side denotes the application of a function to two arbitrary real variables.

    A name that is an abbreviation for a longer conceptual unit can also be hazardous, especially when the resulting abbreviation is just plain confusing. For example, a programmer who desires a name for a rate of pay entry would be unwise to use the name RO PE, which does not semantically reflect the entity's true value. The temptation, of course, is to think of a heavy cord of intertwined fibers. Other poor choices are

P__ENTRY	strange
RATE	not very specific
R__PAY	cryptic

PAY_AMT	amount to be paid?
RATE_ENTRY	vacuous
SALARY	usually not an hourly rate
RATE_OF_PAY_PER_HOUR	too long
WAGE	not specific enough

Good choices might be PAY_RATE or HOURLY_WAGE. These are good, short, full names.

Words like FIELD_1, FIELD_2, and FIELD_3 should be avoided for still another reason. Suppose that the format of a transaction was changed so that the salesperson identification number became the third field instead of the first field, and the item sold number became the first instead of the second field, etc. The word FIELD_1 must then be changed to FIELD_3, FIELD_2 to FIELD_1, etc. Needless to say, it is highly possible that some occurrence of the word FIELD_3 might not be changed to FIELD_1! Finding a mistake like the printer just made in the last sentence is another problem with such words.

Remember, you should only abbreviate after you have created a full mnemonic name. The chosen abbreviation should not activate a psychological set different from the original name.

Let us assume you have created the lengthy mnemonic name OWNER_IDENTIFICATION_NUMBER and that it activates the correct psychological set. Even though you must abbreviate the name, you should reject such abbreviations as OND or OWN_ID, for they may very well be misleading. A word like ID_NUM is preferable. Admittedly, a good solution to the problem is hard to devise, and ultimately depends on the context of the program itself.

Standard Names and Abbreviations

We encourage the adoption of a full set of standard names and abbreviations for every major programming application. For programmers working on a team or modifying someone else's code, the value of standard mnemonics is obvious. Even if you are a student, your instructor may wish to choose standard names for an assignment to simplify understanding of everyone's program.

A formal set of standard names and abbreviations makes the selection of names easy. If your instructor, customer, or programming manager wants an input record to have the name MASTER, or a value on a graph to have the name Y_COORD, then these are the "best" names to use, for they make a program consistent with established conventions.

If you have no formal set of standard names or abbreviations, informal standard names and abbreviations are often available. In the case of a grading program, names like SCORE, GRADE, or MEAN are illuminating informal standards. Furthermore, programmers have their own familiar conventions, for example:

SUM	For summing elements in an array
ID__NUM	For identification numbers
DENOM	For denominators of fractions
AVE	For averages
ERROR	For error flags
TOTAL__ERROR	For total accumulated error values
EPSILON	For error tolerances

The use of words such as these makes a program consistent with informal conventions.

As for standard abbreviations, a good place to start is a dictionary. C allows names with a break character, and this can make abbreviations easy to decipher. You must make sure that abbreviations are well understood. What better place to start than your dictionary?

Abbreviations and short names are a much more important issue than they appear. Long-winded names are tiresome to type, boring to read, and can upset good program layout. Imagine reading a program with many occurrences of

```
CUSTOMER_IDENTIFICATION_NUMBER
```

when, perhaps,

```
ID_NUM
```

will do the trick. You see, the key is to choose those names that

1. can be shortened easily, and

2. are frequently used.

These are the names that count. The point here is *not* to abbreviate uncommon words or those that can confuse. Compare

```
RUN_AVERAGE   vs   RUNNING_AVE
SUM_REPORT    vs   SUMMARY_RPT
N_CHARACTER   vs   NEXT_CHAR
PLYR_NUMBER   vs   PLAYER_NUM
```

The column on the right is superior because the *familiar* part is abbreviated.

Other Considerations

In addition to finding a proper name for each entity, you should choose names that fit well in the program as a whole. Consider the following pairs of names.

	Name for One Entity	Name for Another Entity	Difference
(a)	BKR_PNT	BRK_PNT	Almost invisible
(b)	LIST_ACTION	ACTION_LIST	Verb versus noun
(c)	GET_CODE	CODE	Verb versus noun
(d)	IDEN	IDENT	Small
(e)	OMEGA	DELTA	Short
(f)	ROOT	DISCRIMINANT	Short and informative

In this table the difference between pairs of names is suggestive of differences in meaning. Entry (a) shows two discrete names, but in a program could you be sure that one is not a typing or keypunching error? In general, shy away from using "close" names.

Entries (b) and (c) suggest that one might represent a procedure, the other a (noun) argument. Entry (d) is odd, indicative of a subtle difference in the programmer's (not the reader's) mind. Entries (e) and (f) are fine—short, informative, full names.

Consider the following four function names, which are taken from an actual program. The names had the following meanings:

Name (Argument)	Meaning
MOVLF(SQ1)	MOVE Left From square SQ1
MOVLT(SQ1)	MOVE Left To square SQ1
MOVRF(SQ1)	MOVE Right From square SQ1
MOVRT(SQ1)	MOVE Right To square SQ1

The programmer, in this case, wrote four functions that required a square on a checkerboard as an argument. The input square was denoted by SQ1, and the value returned by the function was TRUE or FALSE, depending on whether it was possible to move left or right, from or to, the square SQ1 given as input. The choice of names, good on initial consideration, resulted in a series of errors. The programmer unfortunately confused MOVLF and MOVRF. It *literally* took days to discover this mistake.

A programmer should also be sure that all user-defined names exhibit "uniformity." This is also a difficult notion to formalize. In rough terms, all user-defined names that imply similar properties should be of similar form. For example, consider the previous maximum value example. It would be unfortunate to choose the names

    NUM
    NEXT
    BIG__VAL

Even though they can suggest the correct meaning, the names do not follow a uniform coding scheme. A better choice of names is

    NUM__VALUES
    NEXT__VAL
    MAX__VAL

The programmer is especially advised to keep abbreviations uniform.

In a similar vein, consider the following names:

    XX1   why 2 x's
    FNXD   cryptic
    CRDTE   unpronounceable
    FLAG   not informative

These are all unfortunate.

Finally, before using a name in a program, the programmer should also make sure that it is not a system name or a keyword. It is handy to keep a list of keywords and a list of system names.

Let us put it this way.

1. Look at the code (not the declaration) to see if a name works.

2. Rely on context to pick a short name that still suggest the correct meaning.

3. Only if necessary, abbreviate.

RECURSION

Loosely speaking, recursion is a method of definition in which the object being defined is used within the definition. For example, consider the following definition of the word "descendant":

> A descendant of a person is a son or daughter of the person, or a descendant of a son or daughter.

In this definition *all* the descendants of the person are simply and precisely accounted for. A nonrecursive definition of "descendant" that takes all possibilities into consideration would be the following:

> A descendant of a person is a son or daughter of the person, or a grandson or granddaughter of the person, or a great-grandson or great-granddaughter of the person, etc.

In this case, the definition is lengthier and less succinct than the recursive definition. It is interesting to note how dictionaries attempt to skirt recursion in the definition of "descendant." "Descendant" is often defined in terms of "ancestor," whereas "ancestor" is defined in terms of "descendant." The two definitions are, in fact, mutually recursive.

In programming, recursive definitions apply to function and procedure declarations. A recursive subprogram declaration is one that has the potential to invoke itself. In other words, it is defined partially in terms of itself.

The primary point of this section is that in many instances recursive definitions are clearer, more succinct, or more natural, than their nonrecursive counterparts, even if they are less efficient. Recursive definitions often follow naturally using the top-down programming approach. A clear idea of the nature and power of recursive definitions can be a valuable aid to a programmer, especially when pointer structures or treelike solutions are used.

Suppose we wish to sum the elements of an integer array. Simple arithmetic gives us the following equality:

```
SUM (A, n) = A[1]                    if n = 1
SUM (A, n) = A[n] + SUM (A, n-1)     if n >= 2
```

Stated in English, the sum of the elements of an array is the last element plus the sum of the first n − 1 elements. If the array has only one element, the sum is the single element. With these facts in mind, it is possible to write the function SUM recursively, as in Figure 6-9A. Its nonrecursive counterpart is given in Figure 6-9B.

Figure 6-9.   ***Summation defined with and without recursion***

(A) Recursive definition

```
typedef int int_array[100];

int SUM (A, N)
     int_array A;
     int N;
{
     if (N == 1)
          return (A[0]);
     else
          return (A[N-1] + SUM(A, N-1));
}
```

(B) Nonrecursive definition

```
typedef int int_array[100];

int SUM (A, N)
     int_array A;
     int N
{
     int I, TOTAL;

     TOTAL = 0;
     for (I = 0; I < N; ++I)
          TOTAL += A[I];
     return (TOTAL);
}
```

(Note: Figure 6-9A is used for simplicity of illustration. It is not a good idea to write recursive solutions for simple iteration.)

To ensure that the recursive definition of SUM is understood, observe the following analysis of the function subprogram when applied to a four-element array containing the numbers 3, 6, 8, and 2.

Depth of Recursive Calls	Value of SUM
1	SUM(A, 4)
2	2 + SUM(A, 3)
3	2 + (8 + SUM(A, 2))
4	2 + (8 + (6 + SUM(A, 1)))
4	2 + (8 + (6 + 3))
3	2 + (8 + 9)
2	2 + 17
1	19

An example better suited to recursive definition is the implementation of Euclid's algorithm for computing the greater common divisor of two positive integers, M and N. The GCD function subprogram requires an additional integer operator % that returns the remainder when I is divided by J.

The definitions are shown in Figure 6-10. For comparison, a nonrecursive definition for the same function subprogram is also given. The nonrecursive definitions are slightly larger and less clear. The properties of the algorithm are still present, but they are hidden by the looping constructs.

Merely knowing what recursion looks like is not enough. It is also necessary to know (1) if recursion is applicable to the problem at hand, and (2) how to apply it. There are no formal rules in either case, but there are some guidelines. One is that the notion of mathematical "induction" is a close analogy to recursion. Induction is a method of definition in which (1) initial values of a function are defined explicitly (the base step), and (2) other values are implicitly defined in terms of previous values (the inductive step). If the definition given in the second step applies to all elements other than the initial values, then the principle of mathematical induction asserts that the function is (explicitly) well-defined for all values in its domain.

Figure 6-10. *Euclid's algorithm defined with and without recursion*

(A) Recursive definition

```
int GCD (M, N)
     int M, N;
{
     int REMAINDER;

     if (M < N)
         return (GCD(N, M));
     else {
         REMAINDER = M % N;
         if (REMAINDER == 0)
             return (N);
         else
             return (GCD(N, REMAINDER));
     }
}
```

(B) Nonrecursive definition

```
int GCD(M, N)
     int M, N;
{
     int REMAINDER, LO_VALUE, HI_VALUE;

     HI_VALUE  = MAX(M, N);
     LO_VALUE  = MIN(M, N);
     REMAINDER = HI_VALUE % LO_VALUE;
     while (REMAINDER != 0) {
         REMAINDER = HI_VALUE % LO_VALUE;
         HI_VALUE  = LO_VALUE;
         LO_VALUE  = REMAINDER;

     }

     return (LO_VALUE);
}
```

To illustrate the method of inductive definition, consider the sequence of Fibonacci numbers. The first two numbers are both 1, and each successive number in the sequence is the sum of the two preceding numbers. More explicitly,

$$N = 1 \quad \text{Base Step} \quad F(1) = 1$$
$$N = 2 \quad \quad \quad \quad \quad F(2) = 1$$
$$N >= 3 \quad \text{Inductive Step} \quad F(N) = F(N-1) + F(N-2)$$

The step from this inductive definition to a recursive function declaration is small. A function subprogram to generate the nth Fibonacci number is shown defined recursively and nonrecursively in Figure 6-11. The Fibonacci function written recursively parrots the inductive definition and clearly shows the main

Figure 6-11. *The Fibonacci sequence*

(A) Recursive definition

```
int FIB (N)
     int N;
{
     if (N <= 2)
          return (1);
     else
          return (FIB(N-1) + FIB(N-2));
}
```

(B) Nonrecursive definition

```
int FIB(N)
     int N;
{
     int F1, F2, I, TEMP;

     if (N <= 2)
          return (1);
     else {
          F1 = 1;
          F2 = 1;
          for (I = 3; I <= N; ++I) {
               TEMP = F1 + F2;
               F1   = F2;
               F2   = TEMP;
          }
          return (TEMP);
     }
}
```

property of the Fibonacci numbers. While the nonrecursive example uses the same property, it is harder to detect. The additional code required to write the function nonrecursively is mostly bookkeeping. Also note that in the recursive definition, the function subprogram FIB is recursively invoked twice. Without a good optimizing compiler, this double invocation is quite inefficient.

A good deal could be said about recursion, and a good deal of the literature is devoted to the subject. For our purposes, the point is simple. Understand the use of recursion and the translation from a recursive definition to nonrecursive code. You may find that recursion is a valuable addition to your programming skills.

EFFICIENCY

Machine efficiency has been one of the most frequent concerns of managers, instructors, and programmers alike. In the early years of computing, when hardware configurations were small and slow, it was important to use as little storage space or computer time as possible. Since then, digital computers have become more powerful, inexpensive, and fast. Yet there is still frequent concern with the question of machine efficiency because of the need to control programming costs.

The reasons for striving for machine efficiency are not only historic and economic; there is also a certain human element. Programmers take pride in their ability to squeeze out excess lines of code or to use an appropriate efficiency feature, and managers take a natural pride in the speed of their programs or their compact use of storage.

The Real Costs

While we do not at all question the need to reduce programming costs, we do believe that this concern is often focused on the wrong issues. For example, some typical concerns in C programming are the following:

1. Using numerous global variables.

2. Avoiding procedures and functions.

3. Making use of goto's.

4. Writing if statements so that the most frequent conditions are checked first.

5. Updating of variables within an expression.

These rules are intended to save space and execution time, thus lowering costs. Because of the often rather small and local savings afforded by the above techniques, we shall call the efficiency they provide "microefficiency" [Armstrong, 1973]. With the development of inexpensive fast storage and virtual memory systems, the preoccupation with the size and speed of machine code would seem to have been dealt a death blow. Not so! Old habits remain.

The concern with microefficiency has often obscured the really important programming costs. The first issue is to understand the problem completely and make sure that the resulting specification satisfies the user. The second issue is to produce high-quality system design, clear code, and clear documentation. The final issue, and only if necessary, is to produce a fast or compact program.

While microefficient programs do help to reduce overall costs, in the larger perspective, they are usually only a small factor. The total cost of a system includes the costs of promotion, time needed to understand user requirements, the development of clear and acceptable specifications, program writing, documentation, and above all, maintenance. If a proposed programming system is not acceptable to the ultimate user, further development is wasted. If specifications are not adequate, system development is often misdirected and delayed. If there is a failure to recognize exceptional conditions and different solution strategies or if there is a poor initial design, the success of any development effort is undermined. Moreover, program development costs include programmer training, thinking time, coding time, and the time and effort needed to integrate a subsystem into an overall system. Documentation costs include the time needed to prepare reports, figures, and summaries of existing code.

In the life of many large programs, the largest cost factor is system maintenance. Maintenance of an ill-conceived, poorly developed, poorly coded, or poorly documented system is expensive and time consuming at best. More typically, program performance is seriously degraded. Easy maintenance of itself can yield greater savings than microefficient program performance. To control programming costs, we must look in the right places.

Program Performance

There are, of course, many cases where program performance is indeed significant. Perhaps a given program will be run interactively, a given data file may be accessed every hour, or fast memory may be scarce. In these cases, attention should be devoted to the *top* levels of program design where "macro-efficient" techniques can be applied.

It does little good to scatter time and space microefficiencies all over the code if the file and array organizations are not optimal. At an even higher level, file and array techniques will be of little avail if the entire program frequently needs to be restarted because of the errors due to the improper input of data. In such cases, perhaps several sequentially executed programs with local and less severe restraints should be designed and substituted for one large program. At the highest level, if the whole program is more easily handled without a digital computer, all the concern with computer performance cost is meaningless.

A rather significant issue stems from the following observation. It is folk wisdom that 90 percent of the CPU time in a program is spent on 10 percent of the code. If a programmer is faced with program performance demands, the first consideration should be *where* the program is losing its time. Microefficiency can then be spent on this 10 percent of the code.

Finally, if you are designing low-level portions of code and really needs microefficient techniques, caution is still in order. Considerations such as packing characters, using integer codes, or avoiding types can make a program quite machine dependent. Tight, tricky, microefficient code can be almost impossible for another person to understand. These performance savings may in the end raise the cost of program maintenance.

Consider Figure 6-12. Each element of code is designed to select the player leading the first card in a card game. Successively higher bids are represented by successively increasing integers. The four-element integer array BID contains the final bids by each of the four players. The players are numbered clockwise from one to four, and the lead player is the person to the left of the highest bidder. Notice that Figure 6-12A eliminates several lines of code. Would you use it in your card-playing program?

Figure 6-12.   *Code to determine leading player*

(A) Tricky version

```
#define NUM_PLAYERS 4
typedef int bid_info[NUM_PLAYERS + 1];

int      MAX, LEADER, N;
bid_info BID;

{
    ...
    N = (BID[1] / MAX) + 2*(BID[2] / MAX)
      + 3*(BID[3] / MAX) + 4*(BID[4] / MAX);
    LEADER = 1 + (N % NUM_PLAYERS);
    printf ("The leader is player number %d\n", LEADER);
}
```

(B) More natural version

```
#define NUM_PLAYERS 4
typedef int bid_info[NUM_PLAYERS + 1];

int      PLAYER, BIDDER, MAX, LEADER;
bid_info BID;

{
    ...
    for (PLAYER = 1; PLAYER <= NUM_PLAYERS; ++PLAYER)
        if (BID[PLAYER] == MAX)
            BIDDER = PLAYER;

    if (BIDDER == NUM_PLAYERS)
        LEADER = 1;
    else
        LEADER = BIDDER + 1;
    printf ("The leader is player number %d\n", LEADER);
}
```

If you do prefer the program of Figure 6-12A to that of Figure 6-12B, look at both carefully. Do you prefer the first because it executes more rapidly or requires less storage? On the computer you regularly use, you may, in fact, find that Figure 6-12B requires less storage, because the loop may take fewer instructions than the straightline code from the corresponding statement in Figure 6-12A. In addition, Figure 6-12B may execute faster because no divisions or multiplications are required, and there may be fewer additions. In short, beware of "clever" code, and beware of being penny-wise and pound-foolish.

The overriding points of our discussion can be summarized as follows. The concern with program microefficiency is often shortsighted. The primary concern should be to consider overall program costs and to place major economic emphasis on earlier phases of program development. There is a lot of money being wasted in the production of poor definitions, poor designs, poor documentation, and in the development of slipshod programs.

And last, but not least, if someone presents a solution that is supposed to be efficient, be careful. Watch out for the rhetoric. Have a live, running demonstration. It's worth a thousand words.

THE CASE AGAINST PROGRAM FLOWCHARTS

In 1947, H.H. Goldstine and J. von Neumann [see Goldstine and von Neumann, 1963] introduced a pictorial notation called a "flow diagram." Its purpose was to facilitate the translation of algorithms into machine language programs. The flow diagrams pictured the course of machine control through a sequence of steps and indicated the contents and change of items in storage. Since then these ideas and notations, along with various diagrams and charts used in business systems analysis [Cougar, 1973], have been absorbed into almost all areas of electronic data processing. The basic concept has come to be known as "flowcharting." We can roughly distinguish between three types of flowcharts: system flowcharts, design diagrams, and program flowcharts.

System flowcharts describe the flow of major data items and the control sequence of major operations in a system. It is customary to picture the relationship existing between information, media, equipment, equipment operations, and manual operations. An example is given in Figure 6-13. There are few specific details, and only a rough picture of the overall process.

Figure 6-13. *A system flowchart for end-of-month weather analysis*

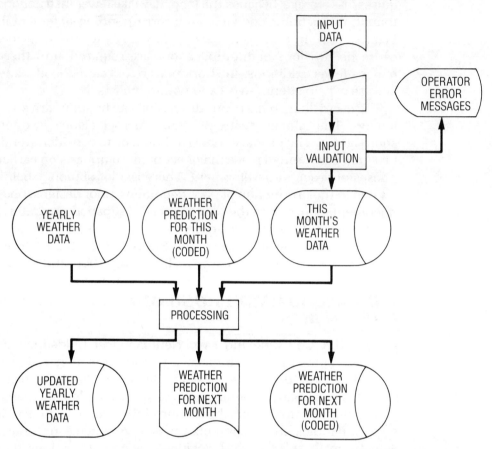

Another example, but more of a design diagram, is Figure 6-14. This suggests a broad view of an overall design. It is quick and to the point.

Program flowcharts, on the other hand, specify details of the sequential flow of control through an actual program. A familiar example is Figure 6-15. Program flowcharts are the most direct descendant of Goldstine and von Neumann's flow diagrams, for both describe the flow of control in great detail. It is interesting to note that program flowcharts do not explicitly describe the data flow, as was the case with the original flow diagrams.

As for system flowcharts and design diagrams, we believe that they can be useful aids in describing systems and processes. For documentation, they can give a quick synopsis of a process. Unfortunately, the use of these charts has sometimes been mistaken for complete problem description.

Figure 6-14.   *Overall design chart*

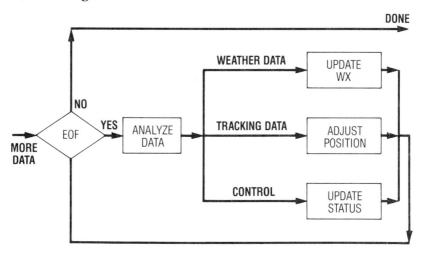

Our concern here is with program flowcharts, a technique familiar to all programmers and one often used daily. It is perhaps true that program flowcharts can assist in the design of very efficient, small algorithms. However, we believe that program flowcharts can easily suppress much useful information in favor of highlighting sequential control flow, something which distracts the programmer from the important functional relationship in the overall design. This, in turn, may obscure the use of alternative designs via the use of procedures and subprograms, the use of more intuitive data structures, or even the simple fine tuning of logic.

The program flowchart in Figure 6-15 may illustrate further the rationale for Proverb 11: Don't Goto. It is simple, but has no meaning without the program itself. Yet the shelves of books on programming are crammed with these kinds of flowcharts—many of the books for novices who are experiencing the delights of their first home computer. Is this representation useful? Perhaps it gives a visual presentation of how data is being determined, but can anyone use the flowchart itself to make a decision about the proper sequencing for coding? I think not. And as more complicated procedures are "flowcharted," a labyrinth of lines, arrows, and geometric figures results in a stillborn challenge just to interpret the flowchart itself, never mind the waste of energy in producing it. Seldom is any meaningful intelligence produced with these kinds of devices.

Figure 6-15.   *A program flowchart*

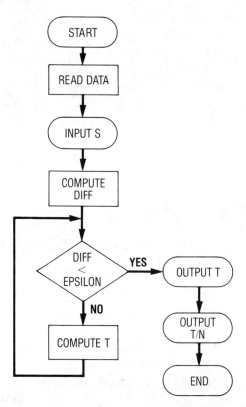

Consider another example, that in Figure 6-16. The a_1 stands for certain actions (e.g., assignments or procedure calls); the d_1 stands for decisions. The programmer who derived this flowchart was so concerned with lines and boxes (i.e., sequences of steps) that the resulting code, while correct, tends to obscure the overall functional logic.

Perhaps the inherent problem of program flowcharts is keeping track of variables that change from one part of the flowchart to the next. A user who is so preoccupied with the flow of control details misses other critical details.

Figure 6-16. **A program flowchart plan**

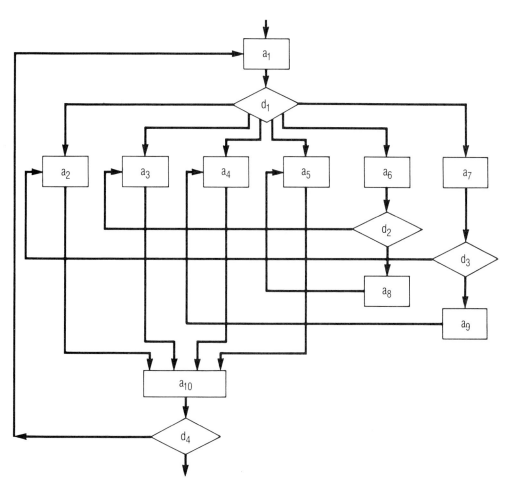

The value of flowcharts is easily discounted. Think back. Have you *ever* been asked to update or correct a program in which the documentation included program flowcharts? Did you consult the flowcharts before updating? Almost without exception our observations and experiences have been that during maintenance and modification of programs, flowcharts are discarded by the necessity of a careful study of the code that produced them in the first place. Code alone is sufficient for any detailed understanding needed for program maintenance.

Another criticism of program flowcharts is the ungainly way in which they always seem to spill over the margin of the paper so that with the many connectors and page turns, you seldom know where you are much less where you are going. Even when the connectors are kept to a minimum to prevent mental page turning, the mental data processing involves too many conditional checks (i.e., branches) in flowcharts. As you connect all these branches to their logical destinations, you are overwhelmed by a "spaghetti effect"—the profusion of so many crisscrossing branches.

Furthermore, if we modify a piece of code, what should be done with the program flowchart? Now we get into a process of revising more lines and boxes, perhaps inventing a color code for "Mod1" and "Mod2". If an original program is truly viable—that is, having the ability to grow and expand—the accompanying program flowchart must be modified as the program coding is changed. After a few years and many modifications, one may have an interesting, modernistic work of art but a doubtfully useful flowchart. Even if a flowchart generator is available as modifications are made, I have found that flowchart generators do not produce a more helpful flowchart for future use than the original one was for the current modification.

In summary, if we look at the various stages of the programming process, the utility of program flowcharts has no meaning in development, documentation, coding, testing, and debugging. And I believe that program flowcharts have a negative effect in maintenance and modification. Simply put, why do we devote talent and energy to something that we do not trust? Programmers and managers should think twice before using time and resources for constructing program flowcharts, no matter what part of the programming process they are designed for. For good program design, we recommend the top-down approach, which is discussed in Chapter 7.

EXERCISES FOR PART II

Exercise 1 *Mnemonic Identifiers*

In creating identifiers, the programmer must guard against using identifiers whose relationships with their values is vague, tenuous, or peculiar to the programmer himself. The purpose of the following program segment has been obscured by the use of mnemonic identifiers and intermediate variables that appear reasonable at first glance but that are, in fact, misleading and confusing. State the purpose of this segment. What quantity is represented by "INTER"? Rewrite the segment using a better choice of mnemonic identifiers and intermediate variables

```c
/* program TRICKYNAMES */
#include <stdio.h>

float NUM, DENOM, SLOPE, INTER;
float A[2][2];
int ROW, COL;

main ()
{
    printf ("Enter values: ");
    for (ROW = 0; ROW < 2; ++ROW)
        for (COL = 0; COL < 2; ++COL)
        scanf ("%f", &A[ROW][COL]);

    if (A[0][0] == A[1][0])
        printf ("NO VALUE\n");
    else {
        NUM   = A[1][1] - A[0][1];
        DENOM = A[1][0] - A[0][0];
        SLOPE = NUM / DENOM;
        INTER = A[0][1] - SLOPE * A[0][0];
        printf ("The answer is %f\n", INTER);
    }
}
```

Exercise 2   *Use of Psychologically "Distant" Identifiers*

Consider the following program specification:

Input: three pairs of integers denoting the coordinates of three points on a grid.

Output: the area of the triangle defined by the three points.

Write such a program using *only* single character identifiers A, B, C, . . .

Exercise 3   *Global Variables*

What is printed by the following piece of code?

```
/* program TROUBLES */
#include <stdio.h>

int A;

int G(X)
    int X;
{
    A = 2 * (X + 1);
    return (A);
}

int F(X)
    int X;
{
    A = X + G(X);
    return (2 * A);
}

main ()
{
    A = 1;
    A = F(F(2)) + A;
    printf ("%d\n", A);
}
```

Exercise 4   *Disagreement*

It is likely that you disagree strongly with at least one of the points raised in this chapter. Pick the one that you disagree with the most and prepare a comprehensive counterproposal. After the customary number of rewrites, have someone else read it. (Hint: Choose a friend to do the reading.)

Exercise 5   *An Essay*

Below are two advanced topics that we would have liked to discuss in this chapter. Pick the one that interests you the most, discuss the relevant issues, seek out the opinions of others, and present proposals which resolve some of the problems therein.

Topic 1: The Problem with Problem Definitions

Issues: How should one detail inputs and outputs? What constitutes a "complete" definition? How much of a definition can be used for documentation? Where do implementation requirements go? What about condition-action lists versus decision tables? How should the layout and organization of a good, complete definition appear?

Topic 2: The Global Variable Problem

Issues: Should C limit the use of global variables? What changes would you make in C to encourage better isolation of modules?

Exercise 6   ## Mr. Croak

There once was a frog named Mr. Croak, who was beset with three daughters of marriageable age, Ribbit1, Ribbit2, and Ribbit3. Now the only eligible male frog, Horatio, fell for Ribbit2 and proceeded to ask for her leg in marriage. However, Mr. Croak, concerned with the marriage prospects for Ribbit1 and Ribbit3, proposed the following: Whichever one of his daughters leaped the farthest would become Horatio's wife.

Now Horatio knew, but Mr. Croak didn't, that Ribbit1 could jump three lily pads, that Ribbit2 could jump twice as far as Ribbit1, and that Ribbit3 could jump only one third as far as Ribbit2. Thus Horatio readily agreed and persuaded Mr. Croak that the following computer program should determine who would wed him. (Note: HEIGHT_RIB1, HEIGHT_RIB2, and HEIGHT_RIB3 denote the heights of the jumps of Ribbits 1, 2, and 3.

```
/* program RIBBITS */
#include <stdio.h>

float HEIGHT_RIB1, HEIGHT_RIB2, HEIGHT_RIB3;

float F(X)
    float *X;
{
    *X = 2 * *X;
    return (*X);
}

float G(X)
    float *X;
{
    *X = (1.0/3.0) * *X;
    return (*X);
}

main ()
{
    HEIGHT_RIB1 = 3;
    HEIGHT_RIB2 = F(&HEIGHT_RIB1);
    HEIGHT_RIB3 = G(&HEIGHT_RIB2);

    printf ("RIBBIT1 = %g, RIBBIT2 = %g, RIBBIT3 = %g\n",
            HEIGHT_RIB1,  HEIGHT_RIB2,  HEIGHT_RIB3);
}
```

What is the moral of the story?

P A R T

THREE

THE PROVERBS IN
ACTION

---

7 TOP-DOWN PROGRAMMING: THE PROVERBS IN ACTION

The play's the thing.

Shakespeare
Hamlet, II, 2

A PROGRAMMER'S CHRISTMAS WORKSHOP

Act 1 (The Problem)

NARRATOR: This is not a fantasy or a play contrived solely for entertainment (although any applause will be graciously received). The play is about a problem and how it is defined, studied, and resolved using the top-down approach for programming. Implicitly and explicitly, the twenty-four proverbs for programming can be found operating in this little scenario. We hope the reader will be pleasantly surprised to see the proverbs in action. So, let the play begin!

Scene 1

[A corporate office. It is late afternoon in early May. Sam is sitting, staring at a blank but lighted terminal screen. The door opens. Walter enters.]

SAM: Walter . . . what news from the iron tower?

WALTER: Christmas is coming.

SAM: A four-hour meeting to tell me that?

WALTER: You may not make it home for the celebration.

SAM: *[Slumping deeper in his chair]* What is it this time?

WALTER: Samuel, I have been appointed to assign you the task of developing this year's most sought-after computer game: Kriegspiel Checkers!

SAM: *[Standing and wide-eyed]* WHATspiel checkers?!

WALTER: KRIEGspiel checkers! And just in time for Christmas!

Scene 2

[It is evening. Sam is home, slouched in a recliner chair in his den. He is reading from a pamphlet titled: The International Rules and Conventions for Kriegspiel Checkers. Tossing this aside, he begins to peruse the company's User Requirement Specification (the URS). He reads:]

In Kriegspiel checkers, each player sits in an isolated area, having a separate board containing only his own pieces. Each move must follow the conventional rules for the game of checkers. However, as each player proposes a move, a third person, the referee (in this case, the computer program), tells the player that either

a. the proposed move is legal, and the opponent will be directed to move;

b. the proposed move is illegal, and the player must propose another move; or

c. the proposed move wins and the game is over.

Additional rules under the current Convention to the Rules are:

a. A player may win the game by capturing or blocking all of the opponent's pieces, and he may also win by getting the first king.

b. When a player proposes a legal jump that is part of a multiple jump, the referee informs the player that a further jump is required and the next square must be entered. The player then continues to propose moves to other squares until the multiple move is completed.

The program must "know" and enforce the rules of checkers, that is, ensure that black always moves first, insist that a jump be made when one is possible, verify the legality of moves, and determine when the game is over.

The rules of play are summarized as follows:

a. Black moves first.

b. Players take alternate moves: black then white, etc.

c. A player moves forward only, along diagonal paths.

d. A simple move is one square forward to an unoccupied square.

e. A jump move requires that an opponent's piece lie on the next forward square and that the square beyond is vacant.

f. If one or more jumps are possible for a player, then the move must be a jump move. If a jump can be continued to jump another piece, the jump must be continued.

g. When an opponent's piece is jumped, the opponent's piece is removed from the board. The piece is said to be "captured."

h. The game is won when a player either (1) captures all of the opponent's pieces, (2) places a piece on the opponent's back row (the king row), or (3) blocks all of the opponent's pieces so that none can move (a rare case).

The program must accept moves in a format familiar to the players. A move consists of two numbers corresponding to squares on a standard checkerboard. The first number denotes the square of the moving piece, and the second number is the destination square. The program must also output "messages" based on whether the proposed move is legal or not, requires a jump continuation, or terminates the game.

The program must be operational by September 1.

As an aid, the standard checkerboard numbering system is supplied with this URS.

Figure 7-1.   *Standard checkerboard numbering system*

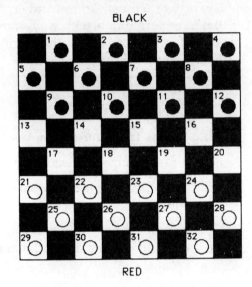

SAM: *[Thinking to himself]* Only Walter could have done this to me. And in ten weeks? Might as well call it Sam's Totenspiel. Looks like the perfect candidate for a top-down approach *[sighing]* — tomorrow.

Act II   *(Program Specification)*

Scene 1

[The office. Three days later. It is morning. Walter enters, pours a cup of coffee, and sits down in a chair beside Sam's desk.]

SAM: Good morning, Walter. What's on your mind?

WALTER: The question is what's on your's—think you can handle the Kriegspiel?

SAM: Sure. But after looking over the marvelous International Rules and the URS, may I pass on some reflections of times past? *[Without waiting for an answer]* Remember that Daytona 500 Race game we did last spring?

WALTER: Who could forget it?

SAM: Right! And you know why we can't forget it? It was a lousy program. Why, you ask? Too many programming delays. And why, again, you ask? Lousy program analysis. We had a lot of time to get on with that program and we still didn't come off with anything sensational. But this time, we've only got eight weeks. And this time we're going to start from the top and work down.

WALTER: What do you propose?

SAM: *[He gets out of his chair and begins to walk in a circle around the desk.]* Walt, let's start by defining the problem better than we did last time. We need to get as complete a functional specification as we possibly can before we set one line of code.

WALTER: *[Picks up the telephone, dials]* Sally—hold my calls for a while.

SAM: *[Restlessly]* May I go on?

WALTER: Sam, I'm interested. You're my top programmer. What I think you're going to say is . . .

SAM: *[Interrupting]* . . . is this. As simple as the inputs for Kriegspiel look on the surface, it's too easy to overlook some of the critical cases involved here. Let me review for a minute. The inputs are a series of pairs of numbers, right? *[Without waiting]* The first number represents the square designating a player's piece, and the second number represents the square to which that piece is to be moved. Of course, some of the pairs representing a move will result in a move that is illegal on a given board configuration.

WALTER: Go on.

SAM: Now suppose that a player inputs a number that doesn't correspond to a piece on the board. Why don't we sit down and make a list of such possibilities—we could call it our "error events list."

WALTER: Good idea. For example?

SAM: Easy. The player makes a simple typographical error—proposes a move that may contain characters that are not numbers at all or inputs a number that is too large to correspond with a numbered square on the board.

WALTER: Two more for the list.

SAM: If we keep the user in mind, we should ask ourselves right now: what kind of errors can they make in using this program? I think it's this kind of human engineering that we missed last time around. Let me ask you how we address these questions. What if the user inputs too many numbers? What if the user accidentally hits a carriage return and inputs no square number at all?

WALTER: Sam, why don't you do this for starters? Make out some kind of a table to spell out as carefully as you can all these kinds of input situations? *[Getting up]* I have to get ready for a budget meeting. I'd like to see what you come up with before we go much further.

SAM: Can do. *[Later that day, when Walter returns.]*

SAM: Behold, sire, I give you a table for Kriegspiel inputs and error messages.

WALTER: *[Looking at the paper. A pause.]* Sam, this is good stuff. I like this "trailing string" input.

SAM: Indeed. Gives the player the opportunity to annotate his game with running comments—after all, who knows when the classical Kriegspiel game is going to be played? Could be lost to all posterity.

Figure 7-2. **Format for input lines to Kriegspiel program**

Input field	Possible values	Error conditions
Normal move (2-squares)		
Leading string	Empty	None
First square number	$1 \leq integer \leq 32$	Number too large or too small; contains a non-numeric character
Separator string	A space or comma	Does not contain a space or comma
Second square number	$1 \leq integer \leq 32$	Number too large or too small; contains a non-numeric character
Trailing string	Any characters	None
Jump continuation move (1 square)		
Leading string	Empty	None
First square number	$1 \leq integer \leq 32$	Number too large or too small; contains a non-numeric character
Trailing string	Any characters	None

WALTER: And now?

SAM: By tomorrow we should have the output messages specified.

WALTER: Any problems?

SAM: I don't think so. The outputs look like fairly simple messages printed to each player . . .

WALTER: *[Interrupting]* . . . along with a display of the checkerboard with the players' pieces . . .

SAM: . . . right! But that's no problem. We'll pass the display problem over to Janet—for us, as Willie Shakespeare would say, "the play's the thing." *[Continuing as before]* There are a lot of possible messages, and I think we should get these in concrete now, rather than coming up with some new innovative message halfway downstream after we start coding. Most of these message requirements are already written into the URS.

WALTER: Sam: some guidelines. These messages have to be short because they're going to be repetitive. And I think that the messages should give the user specific information, especially in those cases where the user makes an error.

SAM: I agree. I should have the proposed output messages for your approval in the morning.

Scene 2

[The office again, two days later. Sam and Walter have been reviewing the first product of Sam's efforts: the proposed output messages and a sample screen layout from Janet's desk.]

Figure 7-3.   *Output messages for Kriegspiel program*

```
Introductory message for player with black pieces
WELCOME TO KRIEGSPIEL CHECKERS.
MOVES ARE GIVEN AS TWO SQUARE NUMBERS, FOR INSTANCE, 9 14

Introductory message for player with red pieces
WELCOME TO KRIEGSPIEL CHECKERS.
MOVES ARE GIVEN AS TWO SQUARE NUMBERS, FOR INSTANCE, 21 17
YOUR OPPONENT WILL MAKE THE FIRST MOVE.

Prompt player for a normal (2-square) move
IT IS YOUR TURN TO MOVE:

Prompt player for a (1-square) jump continuation
YOUR JUMP MUST BE CONTINUED.
ENTER JUMP SQUARE ONLY:
```

```
Acknowledge legal move
OK, YOUR OPPONENT HAS BEEN ASKED TO MOVE.

Non-numeric characters in input square
NON-NUMERIC CHARACTERS IN SQUARE NUMBER.
TRY AGAIN:

Illegal square number
SQUARE NUMBER OUT OF RANGE 1 TO 32.
TRY AGAIN:

No space or comma between square numbers
NO SPACE OR COMMA BETWEEN SQUARE NUMBERS.
TRY AGAIN:

Jump exists and has not been taken
A JUMP IS AVAILABLE AND YOU MUST TAKE IT.
TRY AGAIN:

Illegal move
TRY AGAIN:

Illegal jump continuation
ILLEGAL JUMP CONTINUATION.
TRY AGAIN:
```

SAM: Walt, this took a little longer than I thought. But I thought I should also make a sketch of the input situations to the output responses for Kriegspiel. This gives the programmers who ultimately develop the program the conditions that describe the actions and output response to each action.

[He hands Walter another paper.]

WALTER: *[After reading and comparing the three documents]* Sam, you know what you've done here? *[Without waiting for an answer]* You, sir, have completed the functional specification for user requirements. I simply can't recall if we've ever done it this way before, surely not with the Daytona 500 project. And as such, I say that this is a milestone, almost, in our software development process. What do you say to that?

Figure 7-4.   **Sample screen layout**

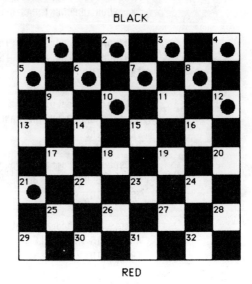

IT'S YOUR TURN TO MOVE: 10 45

SQUARE NUMBER OUT OF RANGE 1 TO 32

TRY AGAIN: 10 15

Figure 7-5.   ***Mapping of input situations to output responses***

Print introductory message to each player, and prompt black player for a normal (2-square) move.

CONDITION	ACTION
1 Game has not been won and a normal (2-square) move is required.	Prompt player for a normal (2-square) move.
1.1 First or second field of input line is not a number.	Print message indicating illegal characters.
1.2 First or second field is a number that is not a legal square number.	Print message indicating square number out range.

1.3 Separator is not a blank or comma.	Print message indicating illegal separator.
1.4 First and second fields are legal square numbers.	
1.4.1 Move is illegal on the current board configuration.	Print message indicating illegal move.
1.4.2 Move is a legal non-jump but a jump exists.	Print message that a jump must be taken.
1.4.3 Move is a legal non-jump and no jump exists.	Print message indicating a completed legal move, process the move, and prompt the opponent.
1.4.4 Move is a legal jump and does not require a continuation.	Print message indicating that a piece was captured and that a legal move has been completed, process the move, and prompt the opponent.
1.4.5 Move is a legal jump and requires a continuation.	Print message indicating that a piece was captured, and process a jump continuation.
2 Game has not been won and a jump continuation (1-square) move is required.	Prompt player for a jump continuation (1-square) move.
2.1 The jump square field is not a number.	Print message indicating illegal characters.
2.2 The jump square field is not a legal square number.	Print message indicating square out of range.
2.3 The jump continuation contiuation.	Print message for illegal jump continuation.
2.4 The jump continuation square is legal.	Print message acknowledging legal continuation and process move.
3 Game has been won.	Print winning and losing messages.

SAM: Would you repeat that to the payroll officer?

WALTER: Very funny. *[Rhetorically]* What next? Before you translate an answer into a pay raise, let me tell you. Documentation. Gather all this stuff together and make a draft for the programmer's documentation manual. Copies to me, members of the operations board, and probably most important, to a few of your colleagues down here. Get their reviews as soon as you can. Remember how we're going about this project . . .

SAM: *[Interrupting]* . . . yes, I know. "Top-down development does not proceed until all the criticism is in."

WALTER: Sam, you've got a good start. You haven't panicked. You've questioned and defined the problem and the documentation will be done as soon as you review the responses you get. You're thinking now. That's good. You can code later. Don't break this top-down approach pattern, Sam. There's always a temptation to hark back to those other approaches that got us in trouble before. Let's not do it this time.

SAM: Right. I think we're off to a good start.

ACT III   *(Top-Down Programming)*

Scene 1

[Walter's office. He answers the intercom.]

VOICE: *[Sally's.]* She's here.

WALTER: Please have her come in. *[Walter goes to the door. It opens before he reaches it.]* Janet! How good to see you again! Please sit down. Coffee?

JANET: Thank you. I hope I'm not late.

WALTER: On the contrary. we weren't expecting you until Monday. *[Pouring the coffee]* All finished now in academia?

JANET: *[With a sigh]* At last! *[Pausing]* And now . . . ?

WALTER: You could not have come at a better time. You didn't meet Sam during your interviews. But you'll be working with him on a new project—Kriegspiel Checkers—has to be done in eight weeks. We've had the URS in hand for a week and Sam's just about finished with the specification. I think, rather than reviewing the status myself right now, and seeing as it's Friday afternoon, why don't I send you on down and Sam can fill you in on the progress. *[Going to the desk, dialing the intercom.]* Sam, Janet is here—I told you help was on the way. Seems like a good time for a briefing on the Kriegspiel before the weekend.

SAM: Good. We'll be all ready for next week.

WALTER: *[Hanging up the phone]* Well, Janet, Sam will be waiting for you. *[In a more serious tone.]* Janet, we have a new challenge here. Sam is an old-time programmer who has been through a lot of programs—some good, some not so good. You'll be working in a different way than you might have learned in college. We think we are going to solve a lot of problems around here with the "top-down" approach—it's really nothing new, just getting back to some basics. Sam has got it rolling now, and you'll have the chance to be on the ground floor of our first effort to bring this approach back to our programming. In many ways, maybe you can lend some new ideas to this effort. Good luck, young lady. *[He shows her to the door.]*

Scene 2

[Sam is alone in the room, seated with his back to the door and does not see Janet come in. She closes the door.]

JANET: Hello, I'm Janet.

SAM: *[Turning in his chair, standing.]* Welcome! I'm more than delighted! I learned a long time ago that sometimes a woman's view of a programming problem has more merit to it than most of us men admit. Mary, who does most of our presentation work, has a knack for it that none of the men, including me, have ever been able to apply to some of the problems. *[Pausing].* So, you're just out of school?

187

JANET: Yes. *[She looks at paper-strewn desk]* And speaking of that, I was trained to keep things as short and simple as possible. This hardly looks like . . .

SAM: Don't let the appearance overwhelm you. You may have been taught correctly. But the complexity lies in the problem itself— we can't avoid that, especially with this Kriegspiel. It is we programmers who are tasked with reducing complexity to manageable simplicity. Let me show you.

[He spends an hour with Janet going over the URS, the principles of the top-down approach, and the work that he has done so far]

SAM: . . . so there you have a brief idea of what the problem is all about and how it should work with this program. What we hope happens here is that now that the specification of the problem has been completed, we won't have to make any programming changes during development or coding. O.K. so far?

JANET: Sounds good. What do want me to do?

SAM: Well, there's not much we can do at 4 o'clock on a Friday afternoon. But I've just finished the functional specifications and I want you to start on the top-down development of the program next week. Why don't you take this with you over the weekend. Monday's my monthly "meeting" day and I won't be here to bother you—that will give you time to see what you can do to get started. The desk over there is yours. *[Pausing as he begins gathering his papers.]* I hope you can lock into this top-down approach as quickly as possible. Remember some of these ideas are relatively new for me, too. And for Walter. Someday when this is all over, remind me to tell you about the Daytona 500 race.

Scene 3

[Tuesday morning. Janet is at her desk when Sam arrives.]

SAM: Well, the early bird! And coffee made already! *[He unpacks his briefcase.]*

JANET: I've made a first pass at the program, Sam.

SAM: Let me fill my cup and have a look. *[With his coffee, he examines the paper.]*

P1 (first pass)

```
initialize program variables
welcome players

do
    get a proposed move
    if move is legal then
        process the move
    if the game is not over then
        change players
    else exit
while not game over
```

SAM: Not bad, in fact, I'm delighted for the second day on the job. Shows some imagination. But . . .

JANET: *[Interrupting]* . . . here it comes.

SAM: *[Quickly.]* No, the first thing around here you'll find is that criticism is not directed toward any one person—criticism is for improvement. Later I'll show all the comments I got when I sent the functional specification around last week. But in almost every case, the critics had something to contribute, and they solved a lot of problems we might have found later—and much to our later regret. So let's take a look at this first pass. *[They sit down together at his desk.]*

SAM: If you have any questions as we go through this, stop so we can both know what the answers are. *[Pausing.]* Three things are apparent. First, you mention the initialization of some program variables but you don't specify which variables are to be initialized and which messages are to be printed. Second, no mention is made of whether a legal move is in fact a part of a jump situation in which the player must input a square to continue the jump. This notation "process the move" is a nebulous subroutine—we'll have to formalize it somewhat.

189

And, third, as you'll find out in the top-down approach, we discard any exits and goto's—nay, all exits and goto's in the program. These clutter a program—maybe not for us—but for the somebody else that is going to read this program someday. So let's see what you and I together can do with a second pass at this.

[In a surprisingly short time, they develop this:]

P1 (second pass)

```
initialize (PLAYER, BOARD)
write (INTRODUCTORY_MESSAGES)

do
      get (MOVE) from PLAYER
      if LEGAL_MOVE (PLAYER, BOARD, MOVE) then
            UPDATE_BOARD (PLAYER, BOARD, MOVE)
            if LEGAL_JUMP (PLAYER, BOARD, MOVE)
            and JUMP_CAN_BE_CONTINUED (PLAYER, BOARD, MOVE) then
                  CONTINUE_THE_JUMP (PLAYER, BOARD, MOVE)

            if NO_KING (BOARD, PLAYER)
            and MOVES_LEFT (BOARD, OPPONENT) then
                  swap PLAYERS
                  prompt OPPONENT for next MOVE
            else
                  write (WINNING_MSG) for PLAYER
                  write (LOSING_MSG) for OPPONENT
                  GAME_OVER is true
      else
            write (ILLEGAL_MOVE_MSG) for PLAYER

while not GAME_OVER
```

SAM: What do you think about this one?

JANET: You first.

SAM: O.K. For one thing, this version calls for one subroutine to check for a legal move and a later subroutine to check if the legal move was a jump and that the jump can be continued. What are we doing with two subroutines? The check for a legal move includes a check for a jump that may need to be continued if it is part of a multiple jump. So why recompute this frequently executed test after it has already been determined to be legal? Why don't we have a single subroutine to check for the legality of the move and return two flags: one that indicates whether the move was legal and the other indicating whether the jump must be continued?

JANET: And?

SAM: And that's not enough. If the move is not legal, one of several messages must be issued. These depend on the kind of error made. I would think that a good way to deal with this situation is to enumerate all possible outcomes. In particular use this: *[He writes:]*

```
typedef enum {ILLEGAL_SQ_NUM,  SQ_OUT_OF_RANGE,  ILLEGAL_SEPARATOR,
              ILLEGAL_MOVE,    JUMP_EXISTS,      MOVE_OK,
              JUMP_COMPLETED, JUMP_CONTINUATION} move_status;
```

Now the evaluation of a move can return the appropriate status value. A case statement can then be used to take the appropriate action.

JANET: Sam, something about the clarity and, to overuse the word, efficiency of the program bothers me. Look here. Passing BOARD as a parameter to almost every function and subroutine seems inefficient. The general use of the BOARD variable is obvious and shouldn't it be passed as an explicit argument to each function and subroutine?

SAM: No, and I'll tell you why. I've heard this argument before and maybe when the program is finished, we can argue about it later. But we want to black-box these subroutines. Although it seems obvious, it's not very efficient. What you're talking about, of course, is global variables, and I don't think you have a case for clarity, either. Spelling out the design in complete detail is what counts now, especially now as we start coding. In the long run, global variables destroy clarity.

JANET: Sam. A question. You've been talking about thinking first—
coding later, black-boxing subroutines, the top-down approach:
is all this something new?

SAM: New? It's been around for twenty years. Walter was in here last
week looking at what has to be done. He's been around a long
time and what he had to say was simply a review of the top-
down approach. *[He mellows.]* It's just that we've been so
caught up in getting a program coded that we haven't been
paying attention to the basics of programming. We forget the
user. We stop reading the literature. And we wonder why
programs crash two days before the deadline. But if we carry
on as we are now, Kriegspie l won't crash. *[Looking again at the
paper.]* For instance, we still have a small error in our second
pass.

JANET: Oh?

SAM: See here? The variable OPPONENT occurs in the code but has
not been given a value. Obviously, the OPPONENT is the other
PLAYER. In addition, GAME_OVER has not been initialized.
These points have to be spelled out. Listen: we can postpone
some of these decisions for the time being about data
representations for the board and players. Some of these
decisions are usually limiting anyway, since there is a tendency
to program around the properties of the representations.

JANET: Shall we try again?

SAM: Why not?

[They are busy once more and produce the third pass.]

P1 (third pass)

```
SET_UP (BOARD)
PLAYER = BLACK
OPPONENT = RED

write (BLACK_INTRO_MSG)
write (RED_INTRO_MSG)
GAME_OVER = FALSE
```

```
    do
            get (MOVE) from PLAYER
            EVALUATE_MOVE using BOARD, PLAYER, MOVE giving STATUS

            switch (STATUS) {
                ILLEGAL_SQ_NUM, SQ_OUT_OF_RANGE, ILLEGAL_SEPARATOR,
                ILLEGAL_MOVE, JUMP_EXISTS =>
                    WRITE_STATUS_MSG (STATUS) for PLAYER
                MOVE_OK, JUMP_COMPLETED =>
                    UPDATE_BOARD using BOARD, PLAYER, MOVE
                    if GAME_WON (BOARD, PLAYER) then
                        GAME_OVER = TRUE
                    else
                        WRITE_STATUS_MSG (STATUS) for PLAYER
                        PROMPT_NEW_MOVE for OPPONENT
                        SWAP (PLAYER, OPPONENT)

                JUMP_CONTINUATION =>
                    WRITE_STATUS_MSG (STATUS) for PLAYER
                    CONTINUE_THE_JUMP using PLAYER updating BOARD
            }
    while !GAME_OVER

    write (WINNING_MSG) for PLAYER
    write (LOSING_MSG) for OPPONENT
```

SAM: Now, dear lady, what do you think?

JANET: I think we've got it!

SAM: Maybe. But let's give it a rest. See you in the morning.

Scene 4

[The office again, next day.]

SAM: *[Looking at Janet as he toys with the spoon in his coffee cup.]*
Something bothering you this morning?

JANET: It came to me last night—and has been nagging me ever since.
It's in this top-level design—CONTINUE__THE__JUMP. It doesn't
make sense. Like the main program loop, it will have to prompt
the player, evaluate moves, and issue diagnostics. It may even

lead to a winning move, yet we haven't taken these possibilities into account.

SAM: I see what you mean.

JANET: We're trying to handle these matters in a subroutine and that is just like writing the main loop again! And what about updating the BOARD again?

SAM: You are saying we have a problem?

JANET: *[Somewhat disconcerted.]* I'm not sure. But I'm afraid now that the way we are handling error messages is not going to work. When we're getting moves, we can find errors in the format. And when we're evaluating moves, we find erroneous play. Can these really be handled together?

SAM: Back to the drawing board? Don't be afraid to start over. Let's see what the next pass will yield.

[After a few hours, Sam and Janet are satisfied at last.]

P1 (fourth pass)

```
SET_UP (BOARD)
PLAYER   = BLACK
OPPONENT = RED

write (BLACK_INTRO_MSG) for PLAYER
write (RED_INTRO_MSG)   for OPPONENT
GAME_OVER  = FALSE
JUMP_AGAIN = FALSE

do
     if !JUMP_AGAIN
          GET_TWO_SQ_MOVE from PLAYER giving MOVE
     else
          GET_SINGLE_SQ_MOVE from PLAYER using CONTINUE_SQ
                              giving MOVE

     EVALUATE_MOVE using PLAYER, MOVE, BOARD giving STATUS
```

```
switch (STATUS) {
    ILLEGAL_MOVE =>
        if JUMP_AGAIN
            WRITE_STATUS_MSG (JUMP_CONT) for PLAYER
        else
            WRITE_STATUS_MSG (ILLEGAL_MOVE) for PLAYER

    JUMP_EXISTS =>
        WRITE_STATUS_MSG (JUMP_EXISTS_MSG)

    MOVE_OK, JUMP_COMPLETED =>
        UPDATE_BOARD using PLAYER, MOVE updating BOARD
        if GAME_WON (PLAYER, BOARD)
            GAME_OVER = TRUE
        else
            WRITE_STATUS_MSG (MOVE_OK) for PLAYER
            PROMPT_NEW_MOVE for OPPONENT
            SWAP (PLAYER, OPPONENT)
            JUMP_AGAIN = FALSE

    JUMP_CONTINUATION =>
        UPDATE_BOARD using PLAYER, MOVE updating BOARD
        CONTINUE_SQ = SECOND_SQ(MOVE)
        JUMP_AGAIN = TRUE

} while !GAME_OVER

write (WINNING_MSG) for PLAYER
write (LOSING_MSG)  for OPPONENT
```

SAM: Just when you thought you had it, you have to do it again.

JANET: All right, but what's so wrong about starting over?

SAM: *[To himself.]* You're learning, I'm learning.

ACT IV   *(Data Representation)*

Scene 1

[The office. The next day. Janet and Sam are having coffee, looking at the standard checkerboard.]

SAM: Janet, now that we've settled on our algorithm, we have to determine what is called "the specific structure of the data representations." All this means is that we have to figure out a way to represent the checkerboard and the player's pieces in the program. It's tempting to code this standard checkerboard numbering system into the program, but the problem is more difficult than it first appears.

JANET: How so?

SAM: First, look at square 10. A black piece on that square can make a nonjump move to squares 14 or 15. So the possible moves are $(10 + 4) = 14$, or $(10 + 5) = 15$, or simply +4, +5. But from square 15 the black moves are to squares 18 or 19, or simply +3, +4. A similar situation exists for red, except that the moves are -3, -4, and - 4, -5, since the move direction is reversed. Now we could sort out which moves use the 3,4 rule and which moves use the 4,5 rule, but we have another problem. Black's first row (squares 1 through 4) uses the +4,+5 rule. But what about square 4? Using the +4,+5 rules, square 8 is a legal square but square 9 is not.

JANET: Sam, maybe I have a solution. I was thinking about just what you have said and I brought in this old article from the *Scientific American. [See Strachey, 1971]*

SAM: Enlighten me, if you will.

JANET: In this scheme, regardless of the square, the possible directed moves for black are always +4 and +5, and -4 and -5 for red. The added border squares are "flag" squares. They contain some value to indicate that they do not represent legal squares. If a proposed move goes from a legal square to a "flag" square, the move will be detected as illegal. The opposite border squares are labeled with the same numbers. This doesn't cause any confusion because they are flag squares and as such will always appear as illegal moves.

SAM: *[After some thought.]* Yes, Janet, this solves a lot of problems. But you know: the players use the standard checkerboard, and the program will have to use this one. This inconsistency means that the input moves will have to be converted to Samuels' representation. This could be tricky.

[Walter enters.]

WALTER: Well, you two seem to be hard at it. A progress report?

SAM: We have settled on the algorithm and we are coming to grips on the board representation. But we don't . . .

JANET: What Sam is trying to say, Walter, is that we need to do some thinking about this before we go on.

WALTER: O.K., but I'm looking forward to a prototype system pretty soon. May I remind you of how many shopping days there are until Christmas?

SAM: Walt, we're close. With a few days for incubation, I think we'll find a solution.

Figure 7-6. ***Alternative numbering for internal representation of a checkerboard***

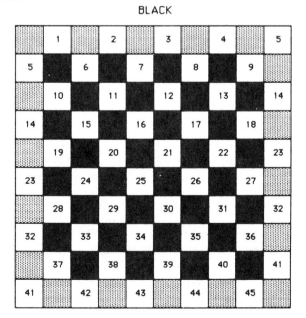

197

Scene 2

[The office, three days later. Janet is at her desk when Sam arrives.]

JANET: Sam, get your coffee and listen to an idea that I have.

SAM: *[He pours a cup, and settles into his chair.]* Do proceed.

JANET: Sam, I've done a lot of thinking for the past few days. It's the board that's giving us a problem, right?

SAM: Right.

JANET: If we think about the board, we should realize that the board has two distinct uses. First, it is a record of the current status of the game. Second, it is a means for determining the legal squares for proposed moves. Aside from the pieces on the actual board, the possible legal squares for a player's moves are constant. Constant, Sam! Why not let the legal square from each square be stored in a constant array? For example—and using the standard checkerboard—for a black piece on square 14, the only possible nonjumps are to squares 17 and 18, and the only possible jumps are to squares 21 and 23. As for the current status of the game, we can maintain a separate array to keep track of the current board configuration.

SAM: I follow all this.

JANET: I drew up this table, Sam. There are some left and right moves that have no legal square, but this won't be a problem because we can always make a special value for this case. For the current status of the board, we can represent the conventional, that is, the 32-square board layout in the form of a 32-element array.

SAM: Janet, you've done it! This is the transition we needed. Now let's see—although this appears easy, there are all kinds of representations for it. With: *[He pauses for a minute then writes on the blackboard:]*

Figure 7-7. *Table of adjacent squares. Dashes represent illegal moves*

Square	Left adjacent square	Right adjacent square	Left jump square	Right square
BLACK				
1	5	6	—	10
2	6	7	9	11
3	7	8	10	12
4	8	—	11	—
5	—	9	—	14
.	.	.	.	.
.	.	.	.	.
31	—	—	—	—
32	—	—	—	—
RED				
1	—	—	—	—
2	—	—	—	—
.	.	.	.	.
.	.	.	.	.
28	24	—	19	—
29	—	25	—	22
30	25	26	21	23
31	26	27	22	24
32	27	28	23	—

type definitions

```
color        enum {BLACK, RED};
direction    enum {LEFT_ADJ, LEFT_JUMP, RIGHT_ADJ, RIGHT_JUMP};
sq_value     1..32;
destination  0..32; /* 0 denotes an invalid square */
```

we could have:

a. One large two-dimensional array

```
type legal_adj_sq
        array [1..64, direction] of destination;
```

b. One large three-dimensional array

```
type legal_adj_sq
        array [color, 1..32, direction] of
             destination;
```

   c. Two two-dimensional arrays

```
type legal_adj_sq
     array [1..32, direction] of destination;
```

```
variables of type legal_adj_sq
     RED_ADJ_SQ, BLACK_ADJ_SQ;
```

   d. Eight one-dimensional arrays

```
type legal_move
     array [1..32] of destination;
```

```
variables of type legal_move
     BLACK_LEFT,    BLACK_LEFT_JUMP,
     BLACK_RIGHT,   BLACK_RIGHT_JUMP,
     RED_LEFT,      RED_LEFT_JUMP,
     RED_RIGHT,     RED_RIGHT_JUMP;
```

   e. A record structure for the possible adjacent squares

```
type adj_sq
     struct {
          destination LEFT_ADJ;
          destination LEFT_JUMP;
          destination RIGHT_ADJ;
          destination RIGHT_JUMP;
     };
```

JANET: *[After she and Sam have discussed the options at some length.]* I think option (a) is confusing and should be rejected.

SAM: I agree. And I think it's time for lunch.

[In the afternoon, they return.]

JANET: Sam—that cafeteria of yours—remind me to bring my lunch tomorrow. *[Returning to the blackboard again.]* It seems in part that the issue depends on whether the PLAYER and the move option (LEFT_ADJ, LEFT_JUMP, RIGHT_ADJ, RIGHT_JUMP) need to be thought of as variables. *[She goes to the blackboard.]* For instance, with an array A of legal adjacent squares and

```
PLAYER = RED;
MOVE   = LEFT_JUMP;
```

one cannot say things like:

```
A_MOVE[SQ]     /* meaning RED_LEFT_JUMP[SQ] */
A.MOVE[SQ]     /* meaning RED.LEFT_JUMP[SQ] */
```

This essentially rules out (d) and (e). It seems reasonable, also, to use a COLOR as an array index. This seems to leave us (b) or (c). But wait, how about a variant of these two choices:

```
type adjacent__sqs
        array [color, 1..32] of destination;
```

```
variables of type adjacent__sqs
        LEFT_ADJ_SQ,   LEFT_JUMP_SQ,
        RIGHT_ADJ_SQ,  RIGHT_JUMP_SQS;
```

SAM:　There seems to be no doubt.

JANET:　Agreed? Now all we have to do is to summarize this in written form.

[They spend the rest of the day working together; this is the product:]

```
#define NULL_SQ 0
#define NUM_SQS 32

typedef enum {BLACK, RED} color;
typedef enum {BLACK_PIECE, RED_PIECE, VACANT} sq_status;
typedef enum {ILLEGAL_MOVE, JUMP_EXISTS, JUMP, JUMP_CONT, MOVE_OK}
            move_status;

typedef short sq_value;      /* 1..32 */
typedef short destination;   /* 0..32 */
typedef struct {
    sq_value SQ1;
    sq_value SQ2;
  } move_pair;
```

```
typedef sq_status board_contents[NUM_SQS + l];
typedef destination adjacent_sqs [COLOR][NUM_SQS + l];

color           PLAYER, OPPONENT;
board_contents  BOARD;
move_pair       MOVE;
move_status     STATUS;
sq_value        CONTINUE_SQ;
boolean         GAME_OVER, JUMP_AGAIN;
adjacent_sqs    LEFT_ADJ_SQ,  LEFT_ADJ_JUMP_SQ,
                RIGHT_ADJ_SQ, RIGHT_JUMP_SQ;
```

SAM: Janet, may I give us each a compliment? I think we've jolly-well resolved this problem. I think we're ready to start writing the main program and—you know what?—I think it's going to be easy.

Scene 3

NARRATOR: The scene returns to the office, a week later. All the while, Janet has been organizing the program as a whole. The main program is shown at the end of the play as Figure 7-8. Let us return to the action!

SAM: *[Seeing what Janet has done.]* Janet, you must forgive my curiosity. I'll have more time to read all this later. But it seems to me that things have been going so well so far; I wonder if you would show me one subprogram—to sort of see if the proof is really in the pudding.

JANET: Why not? Here's the one that was most difficult: EVALUATE__ MOVE. This subroutine takes three input arguments: PLAYER, MOVE, BOARD. It returns a value for the MOVE__STATUS indicator. For a legal move, the following conditions must be met:

-- SQ1 and SQ2 are the part of a MOVE.

1. The moving player must have a piece on SQ1.

2. SQ2 must be vacant.

3. SQ2 must be a left or right adjacent square.

4. If the move is a jump, the intervening square must contain an opponent's piece and SQ2 must be an adjacent jump square.

5. If a jump exists for the moving player, the move must be a jump. The legal adjacent squares are determined by the constant arrays LEFT__ADJ__SQ, RIGHT__ADJ__SQ, LEFT __JUMP__SQ, and RIGHT__JUMP__SQ. The function JUMP __AVAILABLE determines whether a player has a jump.

SAM: Janet, I think we've both learned something. Using the top-down approach, we've been able to define and structure all the procedures so carefully that all of the procedures, as you've just demonstrated here, can be written independently. All the other subprograms will fit the required definitions of the main program.

JANET: So now, Sam, will you tell me about Daytona 500?

SAM: I promise you, you don't want to know.

CURTAIN

NARRATOR: This play, with any suitable change of names and places, is by and large an accurate portrayal of reality. Throughout the play, the top-down approach was, indeed, followed. In all fairness, let us summarize what actually happened.

First, the inputs, outputs, and condition-action mapping underwent many revisions as Sam and Janet wrote the actual program. It would be nice to think that an ideal situation would be that this kind of revision is unnecessary, but it seldom happens.

Second, it was important to alter the move status values and to alter the error diagnostics. In lower-level modules, there were several detailed problems. We consider these as flaws. On programming issues, name changes were made which even affected the main program.

Third, there were debates on the actual kind of error checking performed by the program. This is a difficult issue to address, and the influence of C had some effect on our final compromise. We believe, however, that the lessons demonstrated in this play are applicable to programming in general, regardless of the language being employed.

Finally, there is the decomposition of the program into files. Four conceptual units were defined.

krieg.h   the main program

board.h   all about the checkerboard

user.h   all about the user interface

general.h   a few general purpose constants

Two support files were needed.

board.c   implementation of functions in board.h

user.c   implementation of functions in user.h

This play demonstrates, as do the proverbs, the value of the top-down approach. The overall effect of this little scenario is, I think, to emphasize the importance of thinking, and es-pecially, thinking before any code is written.

For your information, the final program in included in this book as Appendix B.

Figure 7-8.   *Final pass at the main program*

```
main (argc, argv)
int argc;
char *argv [];
{

    CONNECT_TERMINALS (argc, argv);
    SET_UP (BOARD);
    PLAYER   = BLACK;
    OPPONENT = RED;
```

```
SEND_MSG (OPPONENT, RED_INTRO_MSG);
SEND_MSG (PLAYER,   BLACK_INTRO_MSG);
SEND_MSG (PLAYER,   NEW_MOVE_MSG);

GAME_OVER  = FALSE;
JUMP_AGAIN = FALSE;
do {
    if (!JUMP_AGAIN)
        GET_TWO_SQ_MOVE (/*using*/  PLAYER,
                              /*giving*/ &MOVE);

    else
        GET_ONE_SQ_MOVE (/*using*/  PLAYER, CONTINUE_SQ,
                              /*giving*/ &MOVE);


    EVALUATE_MOVE (/*using*/  PLAYER, MOVE, BOARD,
                   /*giving*/ &STATUS);
    switch (STATUS) {
        case ILLEGAL_MOVE:
            if (JUMP_AGAIN)
                SEND_MSG (PLAYER, JUMP_CONT_MSG)
            else
                SEND_MSG (PLAYER, ILLEGAL_MOVE_MSG);
        break;
        case JUMP_EXISTS:
            SEND_MSG (PLAYER, JUMP_EXISTS_MSG);
        break;
        case MOVE_OK:
        case JUMP:
            UPDATE_BOARD (PLAYER, MOVE, BOARD);
            if (STATUS == JUMP)
                SEND_MSG (PLAYER, PIECE_TAKEN_MSG);
            if (GAME_WON (PLAYER, BOARD))
                GAME_OVER = TRUE;
            else {
                SEND_MSG (PLAYER,  MOVE_OK_MSG);
                SEND_MSG (OPPONENT, NEW_MOVE_MSG);
                SWAP (&PLAYER, &OPPONENT);
                JUMP_AGAIN = FALSE;
            }
            break;
```

205

```
                case JUMP_CONT:
                        UPDATE_BOARD (PLAYER, MOVE, BOARD);
                        SEND_MSG (PLAYER, PIECE_TAKEN_MSG);
                        SEND_MSG (PLAYER, JUMP_CONT_MSG);
                        CONTINUESQ = MOVE.SQ2;
                        JUMP_AGAIN = TRUE;
                break;
                }
        while !GAME_OVER;

        SEND_MSG (PLAYER,    WINNING_MSG);
        SEND_MSG (OPPONENT, LOSING_MSG);
}
```

TOP-DOWN PROGRAMMING REVISITED

This chapter presents a technique of program development generally known as top-down programming. The top-down approach presented here is based on the early notions of "structured programming" [see Dahl et. al., 1972] and "stepwise refinement" [Wirth, 1 971]. While the technique is not a panacea for all programming ills, it does offer strong guidelines for an intelligent approach to a programming problem.

Before coding, every programmer must have in hand a complete statement of the problem, a well-planned documentation system, and a clear design strategy. The input format, legal and illegal fields, output files, reports, program messages, and the mapping from all various input data situations to their correct outputs must be described in detail. Furthermore, the overall algorithm must also be determined before coding. It is senseless to start coding a program without such a complete attack on the problem.

The top-down approach has the following characteristics:

1. *Design in levels*. The programmer designs the program in *levels*, where a level consists of one or more modules. A module is always "complete," although it may reference unwritten submodules. The first level is a complete "main program." A lower level refines or develops unwritten modules in the upper level. The programmer may look

several levels ahead to determine the best way to design the level at hand.

2. *Initial language independence.* The programmer initially uses expressions (often in English or pseudocode) that are relevant to the problem solution, even though the expressions cannot be directly transliterated into code. From statements that are machine and language independent, the programmer moves toward a final implementation in a programming language.

3. *Postponement of details to lower levels.* The programmer concentrates on critical broad issues at the initial levels and postpones details (for example, choice of specific algorithms or intermediate data representations) until lower levels.

4. *Formalization of each level.* Before proceeding to a lower level, the programmer ensures that the "program" in its current stage of development is a "formal" statement. In most cases this means a program that calls unwritten submodules with all arguments spelled out. This step ensures that further sections of the program will be developed independently, without having to change the specifications or the interface between modules.

5. *Verification of each level.* After generating the modules of a new level, the programmer verifies the developing formal statement of the program.

6. *Successive refinements.* Each level of the program is refined, formalized, and verified successively until the programmer obtains a completed program that can be transformed easily into code.

One should note several things about the top-down approach. First, the entire problem and its overall solution are presumed to be understood. It is senseless to start programming until there is a complete understanding of the problem and a complete general plan of attack. Such an understanding allows the programmer to write the program without losing sight of the overall goal.

Second, at the upper levels, the approach is machine and language independent. The programmer is not constrained by the details of a programming language. He or she is writing the upper levels using a notation that meaningfully solves the problem, although it might not be understood by a language processor. The programmer's use of a particular notation involves no sacrifice. At each level the statements produced still represent a complete program in some sense. All that is lacking is the machine capable of executing the statement.

Third, at each level of design, informal notation must be formalized as a hypothetical, but explicitly specified, procedure. Specification involves a complete listing of all input and output arguments.

Fourth, at each level the programmer must verify the program in its present form so that further refinements will be absolutely correct with respect to previously designed levels. This usually means running and testing the code already written. The unwritten modules needed for the code are filled in some temporary way. Such dummy modules are called "stubs."

For example, suppose that a programmer is working at an intermediate level and generates the following informal statement:

```
switch day-of-the-week {
      Monday:       generate last week's data summary
      Tuesday:      do nothing
      Wednesday:    update usage file
      Thursday:     process new data
      Friday:       generate lab item reports
      Saturday:     generate weekly breakage statistics
      Sunday:       do nothing
}
```

The language of this statement is far removed from a programming language. On the other hand, the statement is perfectly clear to the programmer in that it reflects a portion of the desired code. The programmer must elaborate on the required inputs and expected outputs for the procedures like "generate lab item reports" and "update usage file." The next levels of refinement must develop each procedure.

The process of solving a problem using the top-down approach is a matter of successive refinements. The topmost level represents the general conception of the problem. At each successive level, the alternative design decisions are exposed. The paths represent all possible correct programs to solve the given problem. At each level, the programmer examines the alternative solutions and chooses the one that appears most suitable. However, if at any time the choice seems unwise, it is possible to backtrack one or more levels and select an alternative solution.

A tree illustrating the top-down approach is shown in Figure 7-9. represents the hierarchical structure of a specific program for which five levels were needed. The top node is the main program, and the nodes at each successive level are the refined submodules that were introduced but undeveloped in the prior level. By the time the bottom level is reached, we have all the modules that comprise the final program.

Figure 7-9.	***Top-down structure for a specific program***

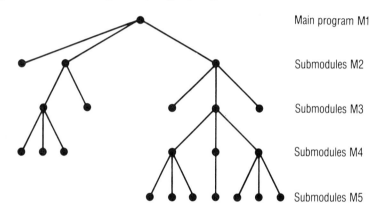

The top-down approach is a programming technique that can be widely applied for good results. The technique does not necessarily guarantee the best solution, but it does provide a good structure for solving programming problems. The play of this chapter has been devoted to an example that illustrates precisely how the top-down method is used to write well-structured modular programs. The example also demonstrates that the method is, by and large, language independent.

EXERCISES FOR PART III

Exercise 1   *Programming Proverbs*

List three ways in which Sam and Janet followed the proverb "Remember Your Reader."

Exercise 2   *Programming Approaches*

Write a short position paper comparing the "top-down" approach with the "systems analyst" approach of Chapter 2.

Exercise 3   *The Input/Output Mapping*

Develop an alternative to the condition-action list method for expressing how a program is to map input situations to output responses. Consider a decision table approach.

Exercise 4   *Program Levels*

Draw a complete tree in the form of Figure 7-9 to illustrate the levels of the Kriegspiel program.

Exercise 5   *Program Modification*

Modify the Kriegspiel program to accept moves in a completely free format, that is, without requiring column placement of the two squares.

Exercise 6   *Program Critique*

List five parts of the Kriegspiel program that, from a quality point of view, can be improved.

Exercise 7   *Speeding Up a Program*

Discuss five different ways for speeding up the Kriegspiel program. If you had to pick one way, which would cause the greatest speedup?

Exercise 8   *Program Development*

Write both an informal and formal statement of the module "EVALUATE_MOVE" for the Kriegspiel program.

Exercise 9   *Program Development*

Following the same specification and top-down development strategy as Sam and Janet's, present a complete program to solve the following problem:

Input:
: A sequence of characters representing the text of a letter. The text contains only alphabetic English words, blanks, commas, periods, and the special word "PP" denoting the beginning of a paragraph.

Output:
: 1. The number of words in the text.
  2. The text given as input, printed according to the following format:
     a. The first line of each paragraph is to be indented five spaces and successive lines are to be left-justified.
     b. One blank is to separate each word from the previous word, comma, or period.
     c. A word cannot be broken across lines.

8 C PROGRAMMERS — WAKE UP

"C is for hackers." That's the oft repeated phrase. That's the image. And then speak to a C programmer. Let he or she tell you about the C code that other people write. Yes, the code is tricky. Yes, the code is unreadable. Yes, the code is dense. The image of the C programmer, you see, is true.

How does the C programmer get this way? For one, C does allow tricky code, and even makes it easy:

- Frequent global variables
- Side-effects in expressions
- Input on the fly
- Easy methods of updating variables aside from explicit assignment
- Intense compression
- Limited type enforcement

But, I submit, programmers can refuse these candy bars. You see, there is another, more fundamental reason:

- C programmers, often used to assembler languages and systems programming, do not appreciate what can be done.

This is the essence of this book:

- YOU CAN, AND SHOULD, WRITE FIRST CLASS PROGRAMS IN C.

You do not have to use Pascal, Modula-2, or Ada to write quality programs. C lets you do it, if you are willing to take the time and thought.

Consider the Kriegspiel program of Chapter 7. The program is packaged into three logically separate units. There are no global variables. No complete module requires a listing of more than two pages of text, and most modules fit on a single page. These characteristics result from human engineering. We all know how difficult it can be to follow a long program. In any lengthy program, we usually try to abstract a logical portion of it that will give us an indication of its overall computation. Every programmer should recognize this fact and write each program so that each logical unit is clearly isolated on a page or two. Furthermore, as mentioned above, each unit should be definable in terms of simple input/output coordinates, avoiding the use of global variables, for these can easily destroy the real modularity of logical units.

Programmers are faced with numerous difficult problems. One point often confused is the difference between problem solving and programming. "Problem solving" [see Lewis, 1980] can be viewed as the act of developing an algorithm to solve a given problem, "programming" as the act of transforming an algorithm into the linguistic concepts of a given programming language. In its conception, this book is primarily about programming, not problem solving. The techniques discussed in it will not necessarily help the programmer find a more efficient method of sorting, a faster method for computing Fourier transforms, or a better heuristic for a chess-playing program.

The programmer's task is usually an intricate combination of both problem solving and programming. The issues in problem solving are vital to writing effective computer programs. Yet it is now well recognized that the "programming" of a given algorithm is far from trivial, and that the programmer should use all the available techniques of programming to ensure that his devised algorithm is clear. While good programming techniques will offer strong guidelines for the development of a good solution to a problem, we must admit that "programming," as conceived here, is only part of the programmer's task.

There are many other issues that need to be investigated. Among these are the need for better training, the establishment of problem definition techniques, and the promotion of human factors. The final issue is the critical need to upgrade the entire programming effort.

With all of the interest in programming, progress is certainly on its way. We must discipline ourselves to this interest but only adopt what is really progressive. Perhaps the best motivation is to recall how much hard work went into the last program you wrote, and also that the program you write today may be the program you will maintain next year.

APPENDIX

A *SUMMARY OF PROGRAM STANDARDS*

GENERAL REQUIREMENTS

[GEN-1] Someone should be appointed to maintain and enforce the standards.

[GEN-2] All full programs shall include header comments.

[GEN-3] For each application there should be an adopted set of standard user-defined names and abbreviations.

[GEN-4] Multiline comments must begin each full line with a double hyphen (--).

[GEN-5] All comments should be written in upper/lowercase.

[GEN-6] Reserved words and preprocessor keywords are to be written in lowercase.

[GEN-7] The words of a compound name are to be separated by underscores.

[GEN-8] No program unit should exceed two pages in length.

[GEN-9] Each function should begin on a new page, or (for short functions) with a break of at least three blank lines.

[GEN-10] Each line should have fewer than 72 characters.

[GEN-11] Each statement must begin on a separate line.

[GEN-12]   Expressions may not produce any internal side effects.

DECLARATIONS

[DCL-1]   All scalars (numbers and characters) that remain constant throughout a program must be named.

[DCL-2]   Variables may not be initialized in their declarations.

[DCL-3]   All types must be named.

[DCL-4]   A (user-defined) function may not change the values of its arguments.

[DCL-5]   The parameters of a procedure should be declared with comments describing the logical role of each parameter.

[DCL-6]   Each field in a record should be declared on a separate line.

[DCL-7]   Declarations may not be used within a nested compound statement.

[DCL-8]   Functions used to return values must have an explicitly declared result type. Functions used as procedures may not return a value.

STATEMENTS

[STM-1]   Goto and Continue statements are not allowed. Except within Switch statements, break statements are not allowed.

[STM-2]   Nesting of any combination of If, For, While, Do, and Switch, statements must be no more than four levels deep. A generalized decision structure simulating a "select-first" is counted as one level.

[STM-3]   Null statements must include a comment line.

[STM-4]   Compound looping statements are displayed with indented bodies. The opening brace is on the header line, the closing brace is after the last statement.

[STM-5]   If statements are displayed in a comblike fashion rather than a nested fashion.

[**STM-6**] The bodies of compound statements, loop statements, as well as the bodies of structures, must be indented from their corresponding header and closing brackets.

[**STM-7**] The + + and -- operations are only allowed in prefix form for solo assignment statements.

SPACING

[**SPACE-1**] A uniform indentation of three to five spaces is to be used.

[**SPACE-2**] At least one space is put before and after each relational operator (for example, =, <, and <=) and after each binary + and – operator.

[**SPACE-3**] A space should be used as in normal English usage.

B FINAL PROGRAM FOR KRIEGSPIEL CHECKERS

```
/* -- Main program file, krieg.c
   --
   -- ** Program Title:  Kriegspiel Checkers
   -- ** Written By:     Samuel Williams and Janet Raymond
   -- ** Date Written:   July, 1986
   -- ** Written for:    Software Development Group
   -- ** Version:        1 (Version 2 will include display of the
   -- **                   board for each of the players.)
   --
   -- ** Program Intent:
   --
   -- This program acts as the referee for the game of Kriegspiel
   -- Checkers. The input to this program consists of a series of
   -- moves taken from two interactive terminals. The output is
   -- the sequence of messages informing the players of the
   -- current status of the game. A copy of each player's pieces
   -- is shown on a standard checkerboard maintained on the screen.
   --
   --                     BLACK
   --
   --              1    2    3    4
   --           5    6    7    8
   --              9   10   11   12
   --          13   14   15   16
   --             17   18   19   20
   --          21   22   23   24
   --             25   26   27   28
   --          29   30   31   32
   --
   --                     RED
   --
   --
```

```
-- ** Rules of Kriegspiel:
--
-- (a) Black moves first.
-- (b) Players take alternate moves: black then white, etc.
-- (c) A player moves forward only, along diagonal paths.
-- (d) A simple move is one square forward to an unoccupied
--     square.
-- (e) A jump move requires that an opponent's piece lie on
--     the next forward square and that the square beyond is
--     vacant.
-- (f) If one or more jumps are possible for a player, then
--     the move must be a jump move. If a jump can be
--     continued to jump another piece, the jump must be
--     continued.
-- (g) When an opponent's piece is jumped, the opponent's
--     piece is removed from the board. The piece is said to be
--     "captured."
-- (h) The game is won when a player either
--     (1) captures all of the opponent's pieces,
--     (2) places a piece on the opponent's back row (the king
--         row), or
--     (3) blocks all of the opponent's pieces so that none
--         can move.
--
-- ** Major Data Structures:
--
-- BOARD gives the status of each of the 32 squares, i.e.,
-- whether the square is occupied by a red piece, a black
-- piece, or neither (vacant).
--
-- LEFT_ADJ_SQ, RIGHT_ADJ_SQ, LEFT_JUMP_SQ,
-- and RIGHT_JUMP_SQ indicate the possible paths that a
-- black (or red) piece can take from a given starting square.
-- There are 32 entries, corresponding to the 32 squares on
-- the board. The values for each entry is a square number or
-- zero (meaning no legal path).
--   For instance
--
--          LEFT_ADJ_SQ [BLACK][17]   == 21;
--          RIGHT_ADJ_SQ [BLACK][17]  == 22;
--          LEFT_JUMP_SQ [BLACK][17]  == 0;
--          RIGHT_JUMP_SQ [BLACK][17] == 26;
```

```
--
-- ** Input and Output Files:
--
-- BLACKS_TERMINAL   I/O device for player with black pieces.
-- REDS_TERMINAL     I/O device for player with red pieces.
-- These are set via argc and argv. */
```

```
/* -- Top level for Kriegspiel checkers */

#include "general.h"
#include "board.h"
#include "user.h"

main (argc, argv)
    int argc;
    char *argv[];
{
    color          PLAYER, OPPONENT;
    board_contents BOARD;
    move_pair      MOVE;
    move_status    STATUS;
    sq_value       CONTINUE_SQ;
    boolean        GAME_OVER, JUMP_AGAIN;

    CONNECT_TERMINALS (argc, argv);
    SET_UP (BOARD);
    PLAYER  = BLACK;
    OPPONENT = RED;

    SEND_MSG (OPPONENT, RED_INTRO_MSG);
    SEND_MSG (PLAYER,   BLACK_INTRO_MSG);
    SEND_MSG (PLAYER,   NEW_MOVE_MSG);

    GAME_OVER  = FALSE;
    JUMP_AGAIN = FALSE;
    do {
        if (!JUMP_AGAIN)
            GET_TWO_SQ_MOVE (/*using*/ PLAYER,
                             /*giving*/ &MOVE);
        else
            GET_ONE_SQ_MOVE (/*using*/ PLAYER, CONTINUE_SQ,
                             /*giving*/ &MOVE);

        EVALUATE_MOVE (/*using*/ PLAYER, MOVE,  BOARD,
                       /*giving*/ &STATUS);

        switch (STATUS) {
            case ILLEGAL_MOVE:
                if (JUMP_AGAIN)
                    SEND_MSG (PLAYER, JUMP_CONT_MSG);
                else
                    SEND_MSG (PLAYER, ILLEGAL_MOVE_MSG);
            break;
```

```
                    case JUMP_EXISTS:
                            SEND_MSG (PLAYER, JUMP_EXISTS_MSG);
                    break;
                    case MOVE_OK:
                    case JUMP:
                        UPDATE_BOARD (PLAYER, MOVE, BOARD);
                        if (STATUS == JUMP)
                            SEND_MSG (PLAYER, PIECE_TAKEN_MSG);
                        if (GAME_WON (PLAYER, BOARD))
                            GAME_OVER = TRUE;
                        else {
                            SEND_MSG (PLAYER,   MOVE_OK_MSG);
                            SEND_MSG (OPPONENT, NEW_MOVE_MSG);
                            SWAP (&PLAYER, &OPPONENT);
                            JUMP_AGAIN = FALSE;
                    }
                    break;
                    case JUMP_CONT:
                        UPDATE_BOARD (PLAYER, MOVE, BOARD);
                        SEND_MSG (PLAYER, PIECE_TAKEN_MSG);
                        SEND_MSG (PLAYER, JUMP_CONT_MSG);
                        CONTINUE_SQ = MOVE.SQ2;
                        JUMP_AGAIN  = TRUE;
                    break;
                    }
        } while (!GAME_OVER);

        SEND_MSG (PLAYER,   WINNING_MSG);
        SEND_MSG (OPPONENT, LOSING_MSG);
}


/* ----------------------------------------------------------------- */
```

```
/* -- Header file board.h
   -- Constants, types, and functions for the BOARD */


#define NULL_SQ 0
#define NUM_SQS 32

typedef enum {BLACK, RED} color;
typedef enum {BLACK_PIECE, RED_PIECE, VACANT} sq_status;
typedef enum {ILLEGAL_MOVE, JUMP_EXISTS, JUMP, JUMP_CONT, MOVE_OK}
             move_status;

typedef short sq_value;     /* 1..32 */
typedef short destination;  /* 0..32 */
typedef struct {
     sq_value SQ1;
     sq_value SQ2;
} move_pair;

typedef sq_status board_contents[NUM_SQS + 1];

extern SWAP    (/* PLAYER, OPPONENT */);
extern SET_UP  (/* BOARD */);

extern boolean JUMP_PATH_FREE (/* PLAYER, SQ, BOARD */);
extern boolean PATH_FREE      (/* PLAYER, SQ, BOARD */);

extern boolean JUMP_AVAILABLE (/* PLAYER, BOARD */);
extern boolean NO_MOVES_LEFT  (/* PLAYER, BOARD */);
extern boolean GAME_WON       (/* PLAYER, BOARD */);

extern UPDATE_BOARD  (/* PLAYER, MOVE, BOARD */);
extern EVALUATE_MOVE (/* PLAYER, MOVE, BOARD, STATUS */);



/* -------------------------------------------------------------- */
```

```
/* -- File board.c
   -- Support functions for the BOARD */

#include "general.h"
#include "board.h"

typedef destination adjacent_sqs[2][NUM_SQS + 1];
/* The 0-th element of the array is unused. */

adjacent_sqs LEFT_ADJ_SQ =
{
    /* BLACK */ { 0,
        5,  6,  7,  8,      0,  9, 10, 11,
       13, 14, 15, 16,      0, 17, 18, 19,
       21, 22, 23, 24,      0, 25, 26, 27,
       29, 30, 31, 32,      0,  0,  0,  0 },

    /* RED */   { 0,
        0,  0,  0,  0,      0,  1,  2,  3,
        5,  6,  7,  8,      0,  9, 10, 11,
       13, 14, 15, 16,      0, 17, 18, 19,
       21, 22, 23, 24,      0, 25, 26, 27 }
};


adjacent_sqs LEFT_JUMP_SQ =
{
    /* BLACK */ { 0,
        0,  9, 10, 11,      0, 13, 14, 15,
        0, 17, 18, 19,      0, 21, 22, 23,
        0, 25, 26, 27,      0, 29, 30, 31,
        0,  0,  0,  0,      0,  0,  0,  0 };

    /* RED */   { 0,
        0,  0,  0,  0,      0,  0,  0,  0,
        0,  1,  2,  3,      0,  5,  6,  7,
        0,  9, 10, 11,      0, 13, 14, 15,
        0, 17, 18, 19,      0, 21, 22, 23 }
};
```

```
adjacent_sqs RIGHT_ADJ_SQ =
{
    /* BLACK */  { 0,
          6,  7,  8,  0,      9, 10, 11, 12,
         14, 15, 16,  0,     17, 18, 19, 20,
         22, 23, 24,  0,     25, 26, 27, 28,
         30, 31, 32,  0,      0,  0,  0,  0 },

    /* RED */   { 0,
          0,  0,  0,  0,      1,  2,  3,  4,
          6,  7,  8,  0,      9, 10, 11, 12,
         14, 15, 16,  0,     17, 18, 19, 20,
         22, 23, 24,  0,     25, 26, 27, 28 }
};

adjacent_sqs RIGHT_JUMP_SQ =
{
    /* BLACK */ { 0,
         10, 11, 12,  0,     14, 15, 16,  0,
         18, 19, 20,  0,     22, 23, 24,  0,
         26, 27, 28,  0,     30, 31, 32,  0,
          0,  0,  0,  0,      0,  0,  0,  0 },

    /* RED */  { 0,
          0,  0,  0,  0,      0,  0,  0,  0,
          2,  3,  4,  0,      6,  7,  8,  0,
         10, 11, 12,  0,     14, 15, 16,  0,
         18, 19, 20,  0,     22, 23, 24,  0 }
};
```

```
SWAP (PLAYER,  OPPONENT)
    color *PLAYER, *OPPONENT;
{
    color OLD_PLAYER;

    OLD_PLAYER = *PLAYER;
    *PLAYER    = *OPPONENT;
    *OPPONENT  = OLD_PLAYER;
}




SET_UP (BOARD)
    board_contents BOARD;
{
    sq_value FIRST_BLACK_SQ  =   1;
    sq_value LAST_BLACK_SQ   =  12;
    sq_value FIRST_VACANT_SQ =  13;
    sq_value LAST_VACANT_SQ  =  20;
    sq_value FIRST_RED_SQ    =  21;
    sq_value LAST_RED_SQ     =  32;

    sq_value SQ;

    for (SQ = FIRST_BLACK_SQ; SQ <= LAST_BLACK_SQ; ++SQ)
        BOARD[SQ] = BLACK_PIECE;

    for (SQ = FIRST_VACANT_SQ; SQ <= LAST_VACANT_SQ; ++SQ)
        BOARD[SQ] = VACANT;

    for (SQ = FIRST_RED_SQ; SQ <= LAST_RED_SQ; ++SQ)
        BOARD[SQ] = RED_PIECE;
}
```

```
boolean JUMP_PATH_FREE (/*for*/  PLAYER,
                        /*from*/ SQ,
                        /*on*/   BOARD)

    color PLAYER;
    sq_value SQ;
    board_contents BOARD;

{

    sq_status OPPONENTS_PIECE;
    boolean PATH_FOUND;

    if (PLAYER == BLACK)
        OPPONENTS_PIECE = RED_PIECE;
    else
            OPPONENTS_PIECE = BLACK_PIECE;
    PATH_FOUND = FALSE;

    if (LEFT_JUMP_SQ[PLAYER][SQ] != NULL_SQ)
        if ((BOARD[LEFT_JUMP_SQ[PLAYER][SQ]] == VACANT)
        && (BOARD[LEFT_ADJ_SQ[PLAYER][SQ]]   == OPPONENTS_PIECE))
            PATH_FOUND = TRUE;

    if (RIGHT_JUMP_SQ[PLAYER, SQ] != NULL_SQ)
        if ((BOARD[RIGHT_JUMP_SQ[PLAYER][SQ]] == VACANT)
        && (BOARD[RIGHT_ADJ_SQ[PLAYER][SQ]]   == OPPONENTS_PIECE))
            PATH_FOUND = TRUE;

    return (PATH_FOUND);
}
```

```
boolean PATH_FREE (/*for*/  PLAYER,
                   /*from*/ SQ,
                   /*on*/   BOARD)

    color PLAYER;
    sq_value SQ;
    board_contents BOARD;
{
    boolean PATH_FOUND;
    sq_status PLAYERS_PIECE;
    destination LEFT_SQ, RIGHT_SQ;

    if (PLAYER == BLACK)
        PLAYERS_PIECE = BLACK_PIECE;

    else
        PLAYERS_PIECE = RED_PIECE;
    PATH_FOUND = FALSE;

    LEFT_SQ  = LEFT_ADJ_SQ [PLAYER][SQ];
    RIGHT_SQ = RIGHT_ADJ_SQ[PLAYER][SQ];
    if (BOARD[SQ] == PLAYERS_PIECE) {
        if (LEFT_SQ != NULL_SQ)
            if (BOARD[LEFT_SQ] == VACANT)
                PATH_FOUND = TRUE;
        if (RIGHT_SQ != NULL_SQ)
            if (BOARD[RIGHT_SQ] == VACANT)
                PATH_FOUND = TRUE;
    }

    if (PATH_FOUND)
        return (TRUE);
    else
        return (JUMP_PATH_FREE(PLAYER, SQ, BOARD));
}
```

```
boolean JUMP_AVAILABLE (/*for*/ PLAYER,
                        /*on*/  BOARD)

    color PLAYER;
    board_contents BOARD;
{
    short SQ_NUM;
    boolean JUMP_FOUND;

    SQ_NUM = 0;
    JUMP_FOUND = FALSE;
    do {
        ++SQ_NUM;
        switch (PLAYER) {
            case BLACK:
                if (BOARD[SQ_NUM] == BLACK_PIECE)
                    JUMP_FOUND = JUMP_PATH_FREE(PLAYER, SQ_NUM, BOARD);
                break;
            case RED:
                if (BOARD[SQ_NUM] == RED_PIECE)
                    JUMP_FOUND = JUMP_PATH_FREE(PLAYER, SQ_NUM, BOARD);
                break;
        }
    } while (!JUMP_FOUND && (SQ_NUM < NUM_SQS));

    return (JUMP_FOUND);
}
```

```
boolean NO_MOVES_LEFT (/*for*/ PLAYER,
                       /*on*/  BOARD)

    color PLAYER;
    board_contents BOARD;

/* -- Tests if all pieces are blocked. */

{
    short SQ_NUM;
    boolean MOVE_FOUND;

    SQ_NUM = 0;
    MOVE_FOUND = FALSE;
    do {
        ++SQ_NUM;
        switch (PLAYER) {
            case BLACK:
                if (BOARD[SQ_NUM] == BLACK_PIECE)
                    MOVE_FOUND = PATH_FREE(PLAYER, SQ_NUM, BOARD);
                break;
            case RED:
                if (BOARD[SQ_NUM] == RED_PIECE)
                    MOVE_FOUND = PATH_FREE(PLAYER, SQ_NUM, BOARD);
                break;
        }
    } while (!MOVE_FOUND && (SQ_NUM < NUM_SQS));

    return (!MOVE_FOUND);
}
```

```
boolean GAME_WON (/*for*/ PLAYER,
                  /*on*/  BOARD)

     color PLAYER;
     board_contents BOARD;

/* -- Checks status of the king row and total blocking. */

{
     switch (PLAYER) {
     case BLACK:

          if ((BOARD[29] == BLACK_PIECE) || (BOARD[30] == BLACK_PIECE)
          ||  (BOARD[31] == BLACK_PIECE) || (BOARD[32] == BLACK_PIECE)
          ||   NO_MOVES_LEFT(RED, BOARD))
                    return (TRUE);
               else
                    return (FALSE);
               break;
     case RED:
          if ((BOARD[1] == RED_PIECE) || (BOARD[2] == RED_PIECE)
          ||  (BOARD[3] == RED_PIECE) || (BOARD[4] == RED_PIECE)
          ||   NO_MOVES_LEFT(BLACK, BOARD))
                    return (TRUE);
               else
                    return (FALSE);
               break;

     }
}
```

```
UPDATE_BOARD (/*for*/      PLAYER,
             /*using*/     MOVE,
             /*updating*/  BOARD)

     color PLAYER;
     move_pair MOVE;
     board_contents BOARD;

{

     sq_value SQ1, SQ2;

     SQ1 = MOVE.SQ1;
     SQ2 = MOVE.SQ2;
     BOARD[SQ2] = BOARD[SQ1];
     BOARD[SQ1] = VACANT;

     if (LEFT_JUMP_SQ[PLAYER][SQ1] == SQ2)
          BOARD[ LEFT_ADJ_SQ[PLAYER][SQ1] ] = VACANT;
     else if (RIGHT_JUMP_SQ[PLAYER][SQ1] == SQ2)
          BOARD[ RIGHT_ADJ_SQ[PLAYER][SQ1] ] = VACANT;
}
```

```
EVALUATE_MOVE (/*using*/  PLAYER, MOVE, BOARD,
               /*giving*/ STATUS)


    color PLAYER;
    move_pair MOVE;
    board_contents BOARD;
    move_status *STATUS;
{
    sq_value SQ1, SQ2;
    sq_status PLAYERS_PIECE, OPPONENTS_PIECE;
    boolean ERROR;

    if (PLAYER == BLACK) {
        PLAYERS_PIECE   = BLACK_PIECE;
        OPPONENTS_PIECE = RED_PIECE;
    } else {
        PLAYERS_PIECE   = RED_PIECE;
        OPPONENTS_PIECE = BLACK_PIECE;
    }
    SQ1 = MOVE.SQ1;
    SQ2 = MOVE.SQ2;

    if ((BOARD[SQ1] == PLAYERS_PIECE) && (BOARD[SQ2] == VACANT))
        switch (JUMP_AVAILABLE(PLAYER, BOARD)) {
        case FALSE:
            if ((LEFT_ADJ_SQ[PLAYER][SQ1] == SQ2)
            || (RIGHT_ADJ_SQ[PLAYER][SQ1] == SQ2))
                *STATUS = MOVE_OK;
            else
                *STATUS = ILLEGAL_MOVE;
            break;
        case TRUE:
            if (LEFT_JUMP_SQ[PLAYER][SQ1] == SQ2) {
                if (BOARD[ LEFT_ADJ_SQ[PLAYER][SQ1] ] == OPPONENTS_PIECE)
                    *STATUS = JUMP;
                else
                    *STATUS = ILLEGAL_MOVE;
            } else if (RIGHT_JUMP_SQ[PLAYER][SQ1] == SQ2) {
                if (BOARD[ RIGHT_ADJ_SQ[PLAYER][SQ1] ] == OPPONENTS_PIECE)
                    *STATUS = JUMP;
                else
                    *STATUS = ILLEGAL_MOVE;
            } else
```

```
                *STATUS = JUMP_EXISTS;

          if ((*STATUS == JUMP) && JUMP_PATH_FREE(PLAYER, SQ2, BOARD))
              *STATUS = JUMP_CONT;
        } /* end switch */
  else
      *STATUS = ILLEGAL_MOVE;
}
```

```
/* -- File user.h
   -- User interface input and output */

#define MAX_LINE_SIZE 72
typedef enum {ILLEGAL_SQ, NO_SEPARATOR, SQ_OUT_OF_RANGE, VALID} input_status;

typedef enum {ILLEGAL_SQ_MSG,      NO_SEPARATOR_MSG, SQ_OUT_OF_RANGE_MSG,
              ILLEGAL_MOVE_MSG,    JUMP_EXISTS_MSG,   MOVE_OK_MSG,
              NEW_MOVE_MSG,        JUMP_CONT_MSG,     PIECE_TAKEN_MSG,
              BLACK_INTRO_MSG,     RED_INTRO_MSG,     WINNING_MSG,
              LOSING_MSG} msg_name;

typedef char input_buffer[MAX_LINE_SIZE];

extern CONNECT  (/* argc, argv */);
extern GET_LINE (/* PLAYER, BUFFER */);
extern SEND_MSG (/* PLAYER, MSG_ID */);

extern GET_ONE_SQ  (/* PLAYER, LINE_STATUS, SQ */);
extern GET_TWO_SQS (/* PLAYER, LINE_STATUS, SQ1, SQ2 */);

extern GET_ONE_SQ_MOVE (/* PLAYER, CONTINUE_SQ, MOVE */);
extern GET_TWO_SQ_MOVE (/* PLAYER, MOVE */);


/* ---------------------------------------------------------------- */
```

```
/* File user.c */

#include "general.h"
#include "user.h"
#include "board.h"
#include <ctype.h>
#include <stdio.h>
typedef FILE *terminal;
static terminal BLACKS_TERMINAL, REDS_TERMINAL;



int DIGIT_VAL (C)
     char C;
{
     return (toascii(C) - toascii('0'));
}



CONNECT_TERMINALS (argc, argv)
  int   argc;
  char *argv[];
/* -- Implementation-dependent routine to connect BLACK's
   -- terminal and RED's terminal */
{
        /*
        1.  Use argv to establish network names for
            BLACKS_TERMINAL and REDS_TERMINAL
        2.  Open terminals for communication
        3.  Clear screens
        */
}
```

```
GET_LINE (/*from*/ PLAYER,
          /*into*/ BUFFER)

    color PLAYER;
    input_buffer BUFFER;

/* -- This procedure obtains a line of input from one of the
   -- players.
   -- The input line is right-padded with blanks up to
   -- MAX_LINE_SIZE characters. */
   -- Note: Assignment of I/O devices is implementation-dependent.

{
    int CHAR_POS;
    char C;
    terminal DEVICE;

    if (PLAYER == BLACK)
        ASSIGN (DEVICE, BLACKS_TERMINAL);
    else
        ASSIGN (DEVICE, REDS_TERMINAL);

    for (CHAR_POS = 0; CHAR_POS < MAX_LINE_SIZE; ++CHAR_POS)
        BUFFER[CHAR_POS] = BLANK;

    CHAR_POS = 0;
    fscanf (DEVICE, "%c", &C);
    while ((C != '\n') && (CHAR_POS < MAX_LINE_SIZE)) {
        BUFFER[CHAR_POS] = C;
        ++CHAR_POS;
        fscanf (DEVICE, "%c", &C);
    }
}
```

```
SEND_MSG (/*to*/    PLAYER,
          /*using*/ MSG_ID)

     color PLAYER;
     msg_name MSG_ID;

/* -- Note: Assignment of I/O devices is implementation-dependent. */

{
     terminal DEVICE;

     if (PLAYER == BLACK)
          ASSIGN (DEVICE, BLACKS_TERMINAL);
     else
          ASSIGN (DEVICE, REDS_TERMINAL);
     fprintf (DEVICE, "\n");

     switch (MSG_ID) {
     case BLACK_INTRO_MSG:
          fprintf (DEVICE, "WELCOME TO KRIEGSPIEL CHECKERS.\n");
          fprintf (DEVICE, "MOVES ARE GIVEN AS TWO SQUARE NUMBERS,");
          fprintf (DEVICE, "FOR INSTANCE, 9 14\n");
          break;
     case RED_INTRO_MSG:
          fprintf (DEVICE, "WELCOME TO KRIEGSPIEL CHECKERS.\n");
          fprintf (DEVICE, "MOVES ARE GIVEN AS TWO SQUARE NUMBERS,);
          fprintf(DEVICE, "FOR INSTANCE, 21 17\n");
          fprintf (DEVICE, "YOUR OPPONENT WILL MAKE THE FIRST MOVE.\n");
          break;
     case NEW_MOVE_MSG:
          fprintf (DEVICE, "\nIT IS YOUR TURN TO MOVE: ");
          break;
     case MOVE_OK_MSG:
          fprintf (DEVICE, "OK, YOUR OPPONENT HAS BEEN ASKED TO MOVE.\n");
          break;
     case JUMP_CONT_MSG:
          fprintf (DEVICE, "YOUR JUMP MUST BE CONTINUED.\n");
          fprintf (DEVICE, "ENTER JUMP SQUARE ONLY: \n");
          break;
     case PIECE_TAKEN_MSG:
          fprintf (DEVICE, "PIECE CAPTURED. \n");
          break;
          case ILLEGAL_MOVE_MSG:
          fprintf (DEVICE, "TRY AGAIN: ");
```

```
              break;
      case JUMP_EXISTS_MSG:
              fprintf (DEVICE, "A JUMP IS AVAILABLE AND YOU MUST TAKE IT.\n");
              fprintf (DEVICE, "TRY AGAIN: ");
              break;
      case NO_SEPARATOR_MSG:
              fprintf (DEVICE, "NO SPACE OR COMMA BETWEEN SQUARES.\n");
              fprintf (DEVICE, "TRY AGAIN: ");
              break;
      case ILLEGAL_SQ_MSG:
              fprintf (DEVICE, "NON-NUMERIC CHARACTERS IN SQUARE NUMBER.\n");
              fprintf (DEVICE, "TRY AGAIN: ");
              break;
      case SQ_OUT_OF_RANGE_MSG:
              fprintf (DEVICE, "SQUARE NUMBER OUT OF RANGE 1 TO 32.\n");
              fprintf (DEVICE, "TRY AGAIN: ");
              break;
      case LOSING_MSG:
              fprintf (DEVICE, "SORRY. . .YOUR OPPONENT HAS WON THE GAME!!!\n");
              break;
      case WINNING_MSG:
              fprintf (DEVICE, "CONGRATULATIONS. . .YOU HAVE WON THE GAME!!!\n");
              break;
      }

}
```

```
GET_ONE_SQ (/*from*/    PLAYER,
            /*giving*/ LINE_STATUS, SQ)

    color PLAYER;
    input_status *LINE_STATUS;
    sq_value *SQ;
{
    int NUM;
    input_buffer INPUT_LINE;
    char CHAR_1, CHAR_2;

    GET_LINE (PLAYER, INPUT_LINE);
    CHAR_1 = INPUT_LINE[0];
    CHAR_2 = INPUT_LINE[1];
    *LINE_STATUS = VALID;


    if (isdigit(CHAR_1) && !isdigit(CHAR_2))
        NUM = DIGIT_VAL(CHAR_1);
    else if (isdigit(CHAR_1) && isdigit(CHAR_2))
        NUM = 10 * DIGIT_VAL(CHAR_1) + DIGIT_VAL(CHAR_2);
    else
        *LINE_STATUS = ILLEGAL_SQ;

    if (*LINE_STATUS == VALID) {
        if ((NUM >= 1) && (NUM <= 32))
            *SQ = NUM;
        else
            *LINE_STATUS = SQ_OUT_OF_RANGE;
    }
}
```

```
GET_TWO_SQS (/*from*/    PLAYER,
             /*giving*/ LINE_STATUS, SQ1, SQ2)

     color PLAYER;
     input_status *LINE_STATUS;
     sq_value *SQ1, *SQ2;

{
     input_buffer INPUT_LINE;
     char CHAR_1, CHAR_2, CHAR_3, CHAR_4, CHAR_5;
     int NUM1, NUM2;

     GET_LINE(PLAYER, INPUT_LINE);
     CHAR_1 = INPUT_LINE[0];
     CHAR_2 = INPUT_LINE[1];
     CHAR_3 = INPUT_LINE[2];
     CHAR_4 = INPUT_LINE[3];
     CHAR_5 = INPUT_LINE[4];
     *LINE_STATUS = VALID;

     if (isdigit(CHAR_1) && ((CHAR_2 == BLANK) || (CHAR_2 == COMMA))) {
         NUM1 = DIGIT_VAL(CHAR_1);
         if (isdigit(CHAR_3) && !isdigit(CHAR_4))
             NUM2 = DIGIT_VAL(CHAR_3);
         else if (isdigit(CHAR_3) && isdigit(CHAR_4))
             NUM2 = 10 * DIGIT_VAL(CHAR_3) + DIGIT_VAL(CHAR_4);
         else
             *LINE_STATUS = ILLEGAL_SQ;
         }
     else if (isdigit(CHAR_1) && isdigit(CHAR_2)
         && ((CHAR_3 == BLANK) || (CHAR_3 == COMMA))) {
             NUM1 = 10 * DIGIT_VAL(CHAR_1) + DIGIT_VAL(CHAR_2);
             if (isdigit(CHAR_4) && !isdigit(CHAR_5))
                 NUM2 = DIGIT_VAL(CHAR_4);
             else if (isdigit(CHAR_4) && isdigit(CHAR_5))
                 NUM2 = 10 * DIGIT_VAL(CHAR_4) + DIGIT_VAL(CHAR_5);
             else
             *LINE_STATUS = ILLEGAL_SQ;
         }
     else if (!isdigit(CHAR_1))
         *LINE_STATUS = ILLEGAL_SQ;
     else
         *LINE_STATUS = NO_SEPARATOR;
```

```
if (*LINE_STATUS == VALID) {
    if ((NUM1 >= 1 && NUM1 <= 32) && (NUM2 >= 1 && NUM2 <= 32)) {
        *SQ1 = NUM1;
        *SQ2 = NUM2;
    } else
        *LINE_STATUS = SQ_OUT_OF_RANGE;
    }
}
```

```
GET_ONE_SQ_MOVE (/*from*/   PLAYER,
                 /*using*/  CONTINUE_SQ,
                  *giving*/ MOVE)


    color PLAYER;
    sq_value CONTINUE_SQ;
    move_pair *MOVE;

/* -- This procedure prompts the player for a jump continuation
   -- square until a valid square number is entered. */

{
    input_status LINE_STATUS;
    boolean SQ_FOUND;
    sq_value NEW_SQ;

    SQ_FOUND = FALSE;
    do {
        GET_ONE_SQ(PLAYER, &LINE_STATUS, &NEW_SQ);

        switch (LINE_STATUS) {
            case ILLEGAL_SQ:       SEND_MSG(PLAYER, ILLEGAL_SQ_MSG);
                                   break;
            case SQ_OUT_OF_RANGE:  SEND_MSG(PLAYER, SQ_OUT_OF_RANGE_MSG);
                                   break;
            case VALID:            SQ_FOUND = TRUE;
        }
    } while (!SQ_FOUND);

    MOVE->SQ1 = CONTINUE_SQ;
    MOVE->SQ2 = NEW_SQ;
}
```

```
GET_TWO_SQ_MOVE (/*from*/    PLAYER,
                 /*giving*/ MOVE)


    color PLAYER;
    move_pair *MOVE;

/* -- This procedure prompts the player for the two squares in
   -- a normal (nonjump continuation) move.
   -- Prompting continues until two valid square numbers are entered. */

{
    input_status LINE_STATUS;
    boolean SQS_FOUND;
    sq_value NEW_SQ1, NEW_SQ2;

    SQS_FOUND = FALSE;
    do {
        GET_TWO_SQS(PLAYER, &LINE_STATUS, &NEW_SQ1, &NEW_SQ2);
        switch (LINE_STATUS) {
            case ILLEGAL_SQ:      SEND_MSG(PLAYER, ILLEGAL_SQ_MSG);
                                  break;
            case NO_SEPARATOR:    SEND_MSG(PLAYER, NO_SEPARATOR_MSG);
                                  break;
            case SQ_OUT_OF_RANGE: SEND_MSG(PLAYER, SQ_OUT_OF_RANGE_MSG);
                                  break
            case VALID:           SQS_FOUND = TRUE;
        }
    } while (!SQS_FOUND);

    MOVE->SQ1 = NEW_SQ1;
    MOVE->SQ2 = NEW_SQ2;
}


/* ----------------------------------------------------------------- */


/* -- File general.h
   -- General language constants */
#define FALSE 0
#define TRUE 1
#define BLANK ' '
#define COMMA ','
#define boolean short


/* ----------------------------------------------------------------- */
```

BIBLIOGRAPHY

[Armstrong, 1973]
Russell M. Armstrong
Modular Programming in Cobol
John Wiley and Sons, NY, 1973

[Brown, 1985]
Douglas L. Brown
From Pascal to C
Wadsworth Publishing Co., Belmont, CA, 1985

[Cave and Maymon, 1984]
William C. Cave and Gilbert W. Maymon
Software Lifecycle Management
Macmillan Publishing Co., NY, 1984

[Chmura and Ledgard, 1976]
Louis J. Chmura and Henry F. Ledgard
Cobol With Style
Hayden Books, Indianapolis, IN 1976

[Cougar, 1973]
J. Daniel Cougar
"Evolution of Business System Analysis Techniques"
Computing Surveys, Vol. 5, No. 3, September, 1973

[Dahl et. al., 1972]
O. J. Dahl, E. W. Dijkstra, and C. A. R. Hoare
Structured Programming
Academic Press, NY, 1972

[Dijkstra, 1968]
Edsgar W. Dijkstra
"Goto Statement Considered Harmful"
Communications of the ACM, Vol. 11, No. 3, March, 1968

[Fairley, 1985]
Richard Fairley
Software Engineering Concepts
McGraw-Hill, NY, 1985

[Goldstine and von Neumann, 1963]
H. H. Goldstine and J. von Neumann
"Planning and Coding for an Electronic Computing Instrument—Part II, Vol. 1" *John von Neumann—Collected Works*, Vol. 5,
Pergamon Press, NY, 1963

[Harbison and Steele, 1984]
Samuel P. Harbison and Guy L. Steele, Jr.
A C Reference Manual
Prentice-Hall, Englewood Cliffs, NJ, 1984

[Jensen and Wirth, 1985]
Kathleen Jensen and Niklaus Wirth
Pascal User Manual and Report
pringer-Verlag, NY, Third Edition, 1985

[Kelley and Pohl, 1984]
Al Kelley and Ira Pohl
A Book on C
Benjamin/Cummings Publishing Co., Menlo Park, CA 1984

[Kernighan and Plauger, 1973]
Brian Kernighan and William Plauger
The Elements of Programming Style
McGraw-Hill, NY, 1973

[Kochan, 1983]
Stephen G. Kochan
Programming in C
Hayden Books, Indianapolis, IN, 1983

[Ledgard, 1975]
Henry F. Ledgard
Programming Proverbs
Hayden Books, Indianapolis, IN, 1975

[Ledgard et. al., 1979]
Henry Ledgard, Paul Nagin, and Jon Hueras
Pascal With Style
Hayden Books, Indianapolis, IN, 1979

[Ledgard, 1986]
Henry Ledgard (with John Tauer)
Pascal With Excellence
Hayden Books, Indianapolis, IN, 1986

[Ledgard and Cave, 1976]
Henry F. Ledgard and William Cave
"Cobol Under Control"
Communications of the ACM, November, 1976

[Ledgard and Marcotty, 1975]
Henry F. Ledgard and Michael Marcotty
"A Genealogy of Control Structures"
Communications of the ACM, November, 1975

[Ledgard and Singer, 1985]
Henry Ledgard and Andrew Singer
Pascal for the Macintosh
Addison Wesley, Reading, MA 1985

[Lewis, 1980]
William E. Lewis
Problem Solving Principles for Programmers
Hayden Books, Indianapolis, IN, 1980

[Marcotty, 1977]
Michael Marcotty
Structered Programming with PL/1
Prentice-Hall, Englewood Cliffs, NJ, 1977

[Strachey, 1971]
Christopher Strachey
"Systems Analysis and Programming"
in *Readings from Scientific American*
W. H. Freeman and Co., San Francisco, 1971

[Strunk and White, 1959]
William Strunk, Jr. and E. B. White
The Elements of Style
Macmillan, NY, 1959

[Weinberg, 1971]
Gerald Weinberg
The Psychology of Computer Programming
Van Nostrand Reinhold, NY, 1971

[Wirth, 1971]
Niklaus Wirth
"Program Development by Stepwise Refinement"
Communications of the ACM, Vol. 14, No. 4, April, 1971

[Yourdon, 1975]
E. Yourdon
Techniques of Program Structure and Design
Prentice-Hall, Englewood Cliffs, NJ, 1975

[— Pascal]
The American Pascal Standard, with Annotations
Annotated by Henry Ledgard
Springer-Verlag, NY, 1984

[—Pascal]
American National Standard Pascal Computer Programming
    Language
ANSI-IEEE 770 X3.97-1983

INDEX